Essentials of BUSINESS MATH

Fourth Edition

C. George Alvey
Professor of Business Administration
County College of Morris
Dover, New Jersey

Gregg Division/McGraw-Hill Book Company

GLENCOE

Macmillan/McGraw-Hill

Lake Forest, Illinois   Columbus, Ohio
Mission Hills, California   Peoria, Illinois

Acknowledgments
The author is grateful to the following reviewers and contributors who supplied valuable expertise during the development of this text: Clara Nelson, Central Piedmont Community College, Charlotte, NC; Doreen E. Stern, Educational Consultant, Yardley, PA; and Frank M. Trubiano, Educational Consultant, Long Island City, NY.

Essentials of Business Math, Fourth Edition

Imprint 1991

Formerly published under the title *Business Math 30, Third Edition.*

Send all inquiries to:
GLENCOE DIVISION
Macmillan/McGraw-Hill
936 Eastwind Drive
Westerville, Ohio 43081

3 4 5 6 7 8 9 10 11 12 13 14 15 SEM 00 99 98 97 96 95 94 93 92 91

ISBN 0-07-053827-1

Contents

Preface

Essentials of Business Math, Fourth Edition, returns to its original title, reappearing as an updated version of the highly successful *Business Math 30*, Third Edition. The emphasis on word problems in virtually every skill builder as well as the need for understanding and the ability to round off numbers and estimate answers, continue as important concepts. A new unit on the use of electronic calculators has been introduced in this edition.

Purpose

Essentials of Business Math, Fourth Edition, is a short course in business mathematics that is aimed at achieving the following objectives.

1. Reviewing the fundamental operations of addition, subtraction, multiplication, and division through practice with computations involving whole numbers, fractions, decimals, and percents.
2. Relating a student's computational skills to typical business problems involving interest, discount, payroll, depreciation, retail selling, and checking accounts.
3. Developing a student's ability to use shortcut methods and to work with speed and accuracy.
4. Developing a student's familiarity with the latest tools for computing in business.

The 30-hour format of *Essentials of Business Math*, Fourth Edition, is also well suited to serve as a refresher or remedial text in work-experience programs; integrated block programs; office simulations; and traditional secretarial, clerical, and office practice classes.

Methods of Instruction

Essentials of Business Math, Fourth Edition, has been designed so that it can be used by students who are working on an individual basis as well as by students who are being instructed as a group.

A duplicatable Basic Skills Survey pretest is provided in the *Teacher's Manual and Key*. The pretest, whether used for an individualized program or for group instruction, enables the teacher to assess the math skills of the students at the beginning of the course and to develop a plan to highlight the skill areas requiring special emphasis.

Organization

The text is organized into 30 units called Skill Builders. A Skill Builder is divided into two sections, each of which takes approximately one half hour to complete. The first section introduces a new mathematical skill or business application. The second section reinforces this knowledge, either by introducing a similar skill or by providing further application of the skill.

All instructional material is clear and succinct. The text is replete with sample problems and detailed, step-by-step solutions. These are followed by practice exercises that reinforce the new skills. Because the practice exercises make use of business situations, students have an opportunity to apply the skills they have learned and to understand their importance in solving particular business problems.

Generally the problems have been arranged to progress from the easier to the more difficult problems. Since word problems continue to be a source of concern, nearly all skill builders contain word problems.

A duplicatable Comprehensive Review is provided in the *Teacher's Manual and Key*. It serves as a comprehensive review of the concepts and skills covered in the text. It can be administered as a final exam to any student who completes the course on an individual basis. It can also be used as a final exam for the whole class.

Because of its organization into discrete units of instruction, its immediate reinforcement of job-related math skills, and its use of challenging material for more advanced students, *Essentials of Business Math*, Fourth Edition, is a remarkably flexible program for providing students, either individually or in a group situation, with the math skills they will need in their business education courses and on the job.

Teacher's Manual and Key

The *Teacher's Manual and Key for Essentials of Business Math*, Fourth Edition, is available without charge to all teachers using *Essentials of Business Math*, Fourth Edition in their classes. This manual includes facsimiles of the pages of the text with answers and detailed solutions wherever appropriate. In addition, it contains six unit tests, a Civil Service and Employment test, the duplicatable Basic Skills Survey, a Comprehensive Review and suggestions to the teacher on how best to use the text-workbook in a variety of classroom situations and with students who have a wide range of mathematical skills.

C. George Alvey

NAME DATE

SKILL BUILDER 1A

Reading and Writing Numbers

WHOLE NUMBERS Our number system is the **decimal, or base 10, system.** It uses the digits 1, 2, 3, 4, 5, 6, 7, 8, 9, and 0. The decimal point separates **whole numbers** (numbers to the left of the decimal point) from **decimal fractions** (numbers to the right of the decimal point). The position of a digit in relation to the decimal point indicates the place value of that digit.

The place value of each digit in a whole number is ten times greater than that of the place to its right. Thus, a digit in the tens place is worth ten times the same digit in the units place, and a digit in the hundreds place is worth ten times the same digit in the tens place.

In numbers greater than three places, commas are used to separate every three digits. Each group of three digits (except the units group) is read as a three-digit number followed by the name of the group to which it belongs.

13,750,245,571 is read as "thirteen billion, seven hundred fifty million, two hundred forty-five thousand, five hundred seventy-one."

Note that a hyphen is used when compound numbers of less than 100 are written in words. In other words, all numbers made up of two number names from twenty-one to ninety-nine are hyphenated.

WHOLE NUMBERS															
Billions Group				Millions Group				Thousands Group				Units Group			
Hundred Billions	Ten Billions	Billions	Comma	Hundred Millions	Ten Millions	Millions	Comma	Hundred Thousands	Ten Thousands	Thousands	Comma	Hundreds	Tens	Units	Decimal Point
	1	3	,	7	5	0	,	2	4	5	,	5	7	1	.

Read these numbers, and then write them in *words*.

Example: *809 Eight hundred nine*

1. 83 ____________________
2. 223 ____________________
3. 5,908 ____________________
4. 17,080 ____________________
5. 32,745 ____________________
6. 114,811 ____________________
7. 324,802 ____________________
8. 1,843,630 ____________________

Read these numbers, and then write them in *digits*.

Example: *Nine thousand, forty-three 9,043*

9. Seventy-one ________
10. Sixty-three ________
11. Two hundred forty-nine ________
12. Nine hundred seven ________
13. Sixteen thousand, two hundred three ________
14. One hundred thirty-three thousand, four hundred fifty-nine ________
15. Five million, four hundred fifty thousand, nine ________

DECIMAL FRACTIONS Digits to the right of the decimal point are called **decimal fractions.** Decimal fractions have a value of less than one. Each place in a decimal fraction is one tenth the value of the place to its left.

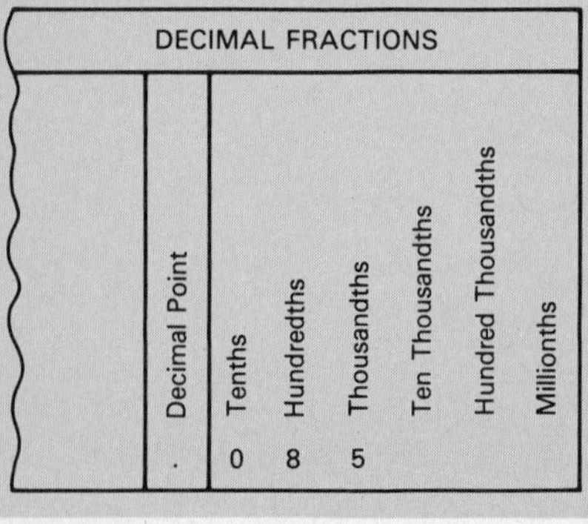

A digit in the hundredths place is worth one tenth of the same digit in the tenths place. A digit in the thousandths place is worth one tenth of the same digit in the hundredths place. Decimal fractions are read as whole numbers followed by the name of the place of the digit farthest from the decimal point.

0.44 is read as "forty-four hundredths."

0.275 is read as "two hundred seventy-five thousandths."

In numbers with both whole numbers and decimal fractions, the decimal point is read as "and."

4.3 is read as "four and three tenths."

18.45 is read as "eighteen and forty-five hundredths."

2.9706 is read as "two and nine thousand seven hundred six ten thousandths."

Read these numbers, and then write them in *words*.

Example: *0.589 Five hundred eighty-nine thousandths*

16. 0.7 ____

17. 0.23 ____

18. 0.68 ____

19. 4.016 ____

20. 5.118 ____

21. 17.83 ____

22. 24.216 ____

23. 3.0808 ____

24. 25.2006 ____

25. 4.00006 ____

26. 379.058 ____

27. 8,016.09 ____

Read these numbers, and then write them in *digits*.

Example: *Sixteen hundredths 0.16*

28. Three hundred seventy-three thousandths ____

29. Eighty-four ten thousandths ____

30. Forty-seven hundredths ____

31. Seven tenths ____

32. Thirty-one and six thousandths ____

33. One thousand, sixty and six tenths ____

34. Twenty-seven and thirteen hundredths ____

35. Three and nine hundred nine ten thousandths ____

36. One and sixteen thousandths ____

37. One and nine hundred thousandths ____

NAME DATE

SKILL BUILDER 1B

Aligning Digits by Place Value

ALIGNMENT Because place value is the governing factor in any arithmetic computation, it is essential that numbers be aligned according to the place value of the digits. When numbers are arranged in a vertical column, the decimal point of one number should be aligned with the decimal point above it. The units place should be aligned with the units place, the tens place with the tens place, and so on.

Failure to write numbers clearly and to align them properly is one of the major reasons for errors in arithmetic computations.

The numbers in Example A have not been aligned correctly. The digit 3 in the first number is in the units place. The digit five in the second number is in the hundreds place. It should have been written two places to the left of the units place, as in Example B. When the numbers are correctly aligned, the correct answer can be obtained.

Example A	Example B
Incorrectly Aligned	Correctly Aligned
3.07	3.07
+500	+500
8.07 ← Incorrect Answer	503.07 ← Correct Answer

Align the following groups of numbers according to place value. Copy them over so that decimal points and digits of the same place value are aligned.

1. 4.72
500
6,843
12.85

2. 0.2705
63
287
10,540

3. 9,453; 9.354; 36; 107

4. 10.057; 9.0003; 12.4; 1,296.46

5. The groups of numbers at the right are from different computer printouts. In the first group, the number zero is printed with a slash through it so it will not be confused with the uppercase letter "O." In the second group, the zero is printed with a dot in its center. Write these numbers in words.

66665	$ 500.00
61Ø26	99.37
355Ø2	105.89
8265	109.87
95238	115.68
54952	123.34

Write the following groups of numbers in digits in a vertical column. Align digits of the same value.

6. Four thousand, fifty-three __________

Six hundred seven __________

Eight thousand, eight hundred eight __________

Seventeen thousand, thirty-two __________

Sixty-four __________

Write the following numbers in digits in the columns at the right. Align them correctly both horizontally and vertically.

Example: *Three and five thousandths*

Twelve and nine tenths

Three hundred six ten thousandths

Forty-two

Sixty and one hundred eight ten thousandths

Ex.

	3	.0	0	5	
1	2	.9			
		.0	3	0	6
4	2.				
6	0	.0	1	0	8

7. **a.** One hundred sixteen

b. Five and six thousandths

c. Thirty-nine

d. Fifty-five and one hundred fifty-one thousandths

e. Eighty-nine and seven tenths

8. **a.** Two thousand, sixty-three and four tenths

b. Sixty-six and sixty-six hundredths

c. Thirty-five and five tenths

d. Six thousand, three hundred twenty-seven

e. Five hundred fourteen

9. **a.** Twenty-seven and three hundred fourteen ten thousandths

b. Seventeen and seventeen thousandths

c. Forty-seven and forty-seven hundredths

d. Nine thousand seven hundred sixty-two ten thousandths

e. Twenty-nine and eight tenths

10. **a.** Nine hundred seventy-two and one hundred twenty-five thousandths

b. Forty-three and forty-three thousandths

c. Fifty-two and five tenths

d. Three and three thousandths

e. Seven hundred six and sixty-seven thousandths

NAME DATE

SKILL BUILDER 2A

Adding Numbers

In an addition problem the numbers being added are called the **addends**. The result of the computation is called the **total** or **sum**. The order in which the addends are added does not affect the sum.

2 + 4 = 6   4 + 2 = 6

CARRYING When adding a column of numbers that totals more than 10, it is necessary to carry the first digit of that total to the next column of numbers.

$$\begin{array}{r} {\scriptstyle 1\,2\,} \\ 939 \\ 147 \\ +265 \\ \hline 1{,}351 \end{array}$$

The total of the digits in the units place is 21. The *1* is written under the column that is added, and the *2* is carried to the tens column. The total of the digits in the tens column is 15. The *5* is written under the tens column, and the *1* is carried to the next column to be added, the hundreds column.

Add the numbers mentally. Then write the sums.

	a	b	c	d	e	f	g	h	i	j
1.	1 7	3 9	5 7	6 4	2 6	8 7	6 3	9 9	9 5	5 5
2.	3 4	6 6	6 8	3 9	1 1	7 9	1 7	2 5	5 6	3 4
3.	1 4 3	6 2 5	8 7 4	5 8 9	2 3 7	6 2 6	9 3 1	5 6 9	3 2 3	6 6 6
4.	1 5 6 8	7 4 4 2	4 1 5 3	5 8 2 4	6 5 7 4	3 9 8 7	2 4 3 5	4 3 6 8	4 4 9 6	8 7 2 7

Some of the following totals are wrong. Cross out any incorrect answer, and write the correct answer beside it.

	a	b	c	d	e	f	g	h	i	j
5.	9 6 8 3 26	7 5 2 6 20	9 8 4 7 27	5 6 4 4 19	3 7 9 3 22	7 9 9 8 33	4 7 6 7 34	9 6 7 3 25	6 4 4 6 20	2 9 9 2 22

	a	b	c	d	e	f	g	h	i	j
6.	17	10	47	70	53	38	45	85	22	31
	21	25	11	19	42	31	22	30	46	32
	41	34	20	20	41	10	51	53	11	66
	79	57	78	109	136	79	108	168	89	129

Add the numbers in the following problems.

	a	b	c	d	e	f	g	h	i	j
7.	89	132	342	45	425	321	1,543	243	2,023	34
	92	88	109	277	231	606	481	1,006	29	930
					456	195	7,328	751	871	256
									530	11

8. Andrew's Art Supplies employs five sales representatives. Each representative's sales during a one-week period are shown below. Find the total sales for each day of that week.

DAILY SALES BY REPRESENTATIVE

REP.	MON.	TUES.	WED.	THURS.	FRI.
Richards	$ 765	$ 875	$1,254	$ 922	$1,135
Wolf	813	934	983	1,268	820
Bookner	906	1,007	834	785	955
Tobin	1,106	843	912	872	1,010
Wood	751	1,254	840	-0-	975
Total					

RECORD VERIFICATION Answers found with calculators are not always correct. Errors can result from copying numbers incorrectly, striking the wrong key, and so on. If a tape is available, verify the total by checking the original figures against the tape produced by the machine. If a display calculator is used, verify the total by redoing the computations.

Check the tapes against the original figures, and correct any errors on the tapes. Then determine the correct total in the space to the right of each tape.

9.

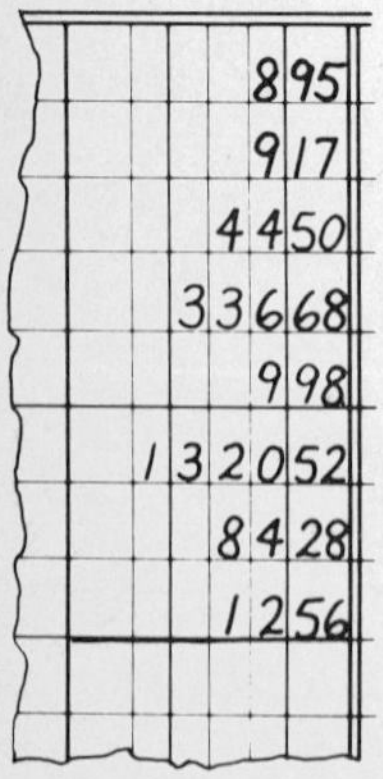

8.95 +
9.17 +
45.40 +
336.68 +
9.98 +
1,320.52 +
12.56 +
1,743.26 T

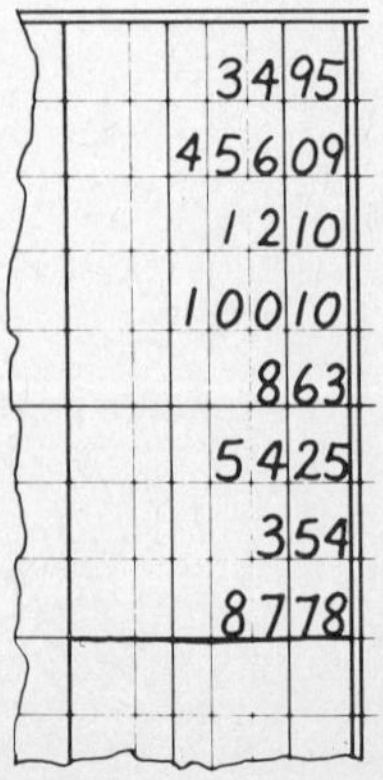

34.95 +
456.90 +
12.10 +
110.00 +
8.63 +
54.25 +
3.54 +
78.87 +
759.24 T

NAME DATE

SKILL BUILDER 2B

Developing Speed in Addition

TWO-COLUMN ADDITION One method of adding two-digit numbers quickly is to mentally add all of the tens digits and one of the units digits first. Then add the remaining units digits to the first total. For example, to add 55 + 83, first add 55 + 80 = 135. Then add 135 + 3 = 138.

$$\begin{array}{r} 55 \\ +83 \\ \hline \end{array} \qquad \begin{array}{r} 55 \\ +80 \\ \hline 135 \end{array} + 3 = 138$$

To add 13 + 49 + 52, first add 13 + 40 + 50 = 103. Then add 103 + 9 = 112 and 112 + 2 = 114.

$$\begin{array}{r} 13 \\ 49 \\ +52 \\ \hline \end{array} \qquad \begin{array}{r} 13 \\ 40 \\ +50 \\ \hline 103 \end{array} + 9 = 112$$

$$112 + 2 = 114$$

Find the sum in each of the following problems. Use the method described above.

	a	b	c	d	e	f	g	h	i	j
1.	26	19	43	79	68	54	99	77	93	84
	57	86	76	44	87	92	32	29	61	39

	a	b	c	d	e	f	g	h	i	j
2.	22	38	57	49	83	19	97	86	46	28
	16	41	35	86	71	99	31	42	59	57
	83	96	48	28	68	67	46	49	32	78

	a	b	c	d	e	f	g	h	i	j
3.	49	42	19	39	68	21	73	59	84	37
	56	61	93	67	86	56	78	67	47	28
	62	98	42	85	40	69	84	82	10	55
	78	48	78	67	69	38	14	66	87	75

	a	b	c	d	e	f	g	h	i	j
4.	75	48	62	41	31	86	56	83	77	81
	15	37	28	60	48	53	20	95	17	62
	53	82	74	39	99	29	33	51	36	42
	98	52	85	58	57	39	68	59	93	57
	84	99	97	75	89	73	99	33	51	29

ADDITION BY GROUPING Another way to develop speed in addition is to add by groups of two or more digits that total 10.

1	2	3	4	5	6	7	8	9
+9	+8	+7	+6	+5	+4	+3	+2	+1
10	10	10	10	10	10	10	10	10

First add any digits in a column that total ten. Then add this total to the remaining digits. In the problem below, the digits connected by lines total 10.

```
          2
         96 }
10 =    54 } = 10
         63 }
10 =    12 } = 10
       +55 }
        280
```

Add the numbers in these problems by using groups that total 10.

	a	b	c	d	e	f	g
5.	216	547	813	5,426	4,875	498	$928.64
	461	164	726	1,251	9,234	953	163.54
	628	432	652	4,943	1,768	691	42.42
	593	634	295	3,942	3,312	462	5.86
	836	522	134	5,627	6,241	312	675.15
						249	12.89
						527	415.32

	a	b	c	d	e	f	g
6.	$9.28	3,613	156	492	333	611	738
	2.86	9,149	904	816	777	994	327
	1.59	2,572	106	329	888	653	673
	4.62	8,426	936	817	222	457	437
	5.43	6,321					
	3.52	4,157					
	6.21	2,212					

Using the methods described above, find the sum of each of the following groups.

	a	b	c	d	e	f	g	h	i	j
7.	427	506	468	683	492	92	955	86	365	513
	68	92	49	91	84	742	91	256	49	47
	127	104	106	121	114	436	484	427	559	562
	653	602	608	801	590	328	379	258	382	432
	371	360	346	294	361	685	764	513	365	607

NAME DATE

SKILL BUILDER 3A

Checking Addition

Never assume that the addition of a column of figures is correct. If figures were copied from another source, check the copy against the original to be sure that the figures were copied accurately. If a printing calculator or an adding machine was used, compare the figures on the tape with the original figures. If a display calculator is used, verify the total by redoing the computations. Check the accuracy of addition done by hand by adding the same figures in the reverse order.

Copy each of the following groups of figures in the space provided, find the total, and then check the total by adding in reverse order. Try using the speed methods presented in Skill Builder 2b.

1.	2.	3.	4.
57	386	$6,321	$54,943
36	159	246	7,156
48	514	2,179	63,041
24	212	1,532	6,119

5.	6.	7.	8.
35	457	15,726	$18,182
16	123	3,168	717
84	316	9,003	4,111
25	286	213	13,155
57	934	1,124	2,435

9.	10.	11.	12.
10,345	6,098	876	$12,387
5,876	23,086	12,432	4,592
11,490	10,137	2,376	5,231
30,467	9,437	690	10,429
3,041	897	4,639	234

13. This record shows the number of bicycles sold during Bike World's sale week. How many were sold each day?

DAILY SALES—UNITS

BICYCLE	M	T	W	TH	F	PRICE
3-speed	5	8	6	-0-	9	$ 84.99
10-speed	11	10	14	12	15	89.99
12-speed	15	16	18	17	24	102.49
20" BMX	4	-0-	3	3	5	69.85
12" RMX	2	2	0	1	7	49.97
Total	____	____	____	____	____	____

14. The Popham Paper Products Company pays its employees based on the number of units they produce in a week. How many were made in one week by each employee?

EMPLOYEE NUMBER	NUMBER OF UNITS					TOTAL UNITS
	M	T	W	TH	F	
31045	65	62	67	61	64	____
10641	63	58	60	61	59	____
42352	54	53	60	59	58	____
10914	68	74	70	76	71	____
91837	59	58	60	60	61	____

15. Evita Murphy recorded her utility and telephone bills from January through June. How much did she spend each month. Double-check your addition by adding from the bottom up.

UTILITY BILLS

ITEM	JANUARY	FEBRUARY	MARCH	APRIL	MAY	JUNE
Gas	$92.53	$102.10	$73.90	$54.35	$35.11	$34.08
Electric	78.14	77.56	74.51	51.28	51.11	46.23
Water	-0-	58.97	-0-	-0-	87.43	-0-
Telephone	23.80	29.75	23.80	23.80	37.18	41.53
Total	____	____	____	____	____	____

16. The Oceanside Community College bookstore held a one-week sale to clear their inventory of outdated novelty items. Find the total sales for each day shown on the sales report below. Check your answer by adding in the reverse order.

WEEKLY SALES REPORT

ITEM	MAY 23	MAY 24	MAY 25	MAY 26	MAY 27
Decals	$58.00	$61.00	$43.00	$49.00	$36.00
Pennants	63.00	70.00	54.25	57.75	49.00
T-shirts	69.00	57.00	63.00	42.00	39.00
Coffee mugs	55.50	45.00	37.50	42.00	15.00
Steins	41.25	46.75	30.25	33.00	33.00
Total	____	____	____	____	____

17. Complete the following production report. Check your totals by adding in the reverse order.

UNIT PRODUCTION REPORT

NAME	JULY 1–7	JULY 8–14	JULY 15–21	JULY 22–28
Sanchez	760	1,212	836	975
Mlynek	685	790	1,005	930
Simpson	725	935	824	1,207
Sumpter	760	1,230	980	874
Woods	770	1,120	915	1,245
Total	____	____	____	____

18. What was the total amount of the payroll for each of the weeks shown below?

NET PAYROLL REPORT

NAME	JULY 1–7	JULY 8–14	JULY 15–21	JULY 22–28
Sanchez	$280.20	$446.84	$308.22	$359.46
Mlynek	252.55	291.26	370.52	342.87
Simpson	267.29	344.72	303.79	445.00
Sumpter	280.20	453.48	361.31	322.23
Woods	283.88	412.92	337.34	459.01
Total	____	____	____	____

NAME DATE

SKILL BUILDER 3B

Adding Horizontally and Vertically

HORIZONTAL ADDITION Often a set of figures is written in a horizontal line rather than in a column. To find the total, the numbers could be rewritten in a vertical column. However, this could be a waste of time and energy and could also be difficult if complex records were involved. The possibility of an error in copying is also introduced. When it is impractical to rearrange numbers in vertical columns, add horizontally.

Horizontal addition is performed in the same way as vertical addition. Each digit is added to its counterpart in each number: units are added to units, tens to tens, hundreds to hundreds, and so on. For example, to add 157 + 316 + 942, first add the units digits: 7 + 6 + 2 = 15 (15 units). Write 5 in the answer space and carry the 1. Add the 1 to the tens digits: 1 (the number carried) + 5 + 1 + 4 = 11 (11 tens). Write 1 in the tens place in the answer space and carry 1 to the hundreds column. Add the 1 to the hundreds digits: 1 (the number carried) + 1 + 3 + 9 = 14 (14 hundreds). The answer is 14 hundreds, 1 ten, and 5 units—1,415.

When adding horizontally, be careful to match the proper digits. Horizontal addition can be checked by adding the numbers in the reverse order.

Add the numbers in these problems from left to right. Check your totals by adding from right to left.

1. 6 + 3 + 4 + 9 + 2 = ________
2. 57 + 19 + 82 + 36 + 96 = ________
3. 5 + 8 + 1 + 7 + 5 = ________
4. 54 + 22 + 10 + 83 + 44 = ________
5. 7 + 4 + 6 + 3 + 9 = ________
6. 99 + 14 + 35 + 23 + 36 = ________
7. 8 + 4 + 5 + 6 + 2 = ________
8. 139 + 643 + 435 + 815 = ________

HORIZONTAL AND VERTICAL ADDITION Many business forms require numbers to be added both horizontally and vertically. For example, the following problems are excerpts from ledgers. The total of all the vertical columns should equal the total of all the horizontal rows. This procedure, called **crossfooting,** is the most positive check for accuracy.

Add the numbers horizontally and vertically. Then add the totals of the vertical columns and horizontal rows.

9.

5	4	3	9	
7	8	1	2	
4	7	9	3	
5	1	6	8	

10.

16	89	57	
45	65	55	
93	22	18	
44	39	56	

11.

1,526	142	901	
803	345	541	
2,000	93	488	
826	329	281	

12.

159	345	80	
1,345	876	1,250	
947	3,222	435	
500	1,303	612	

13. Oliver Products calculates total sales for each day as well as total sales for the week. On the following sales report, find the daily total of all the sales, the total for the week for each sales representative, and the grand total for the week.

WEEKLY SALES REPORT

SALES REP.	SUN.	MON.	TUES.	WED.	THURS.	FRI.	SAT.	TOTAL
Ling	$2,409.	$ -0-	$2,712.	$3,930.	$ -0-	$2,664.	$2,670.	______
Wolf	-0-	3,750.	-0-	2,625.	2,790.	2,889.	3,450.	______
Bookner	2,727.	3,690.	-0-	-0-	3,450.	-0-	2,535.	______
Ameredes	2,295.	-0-	3,855.	2,616.	-0-	2,958.	2,796.	______
Perez	-0-	2,631.	-0-	2,895.	2,205.	3,600.	2,682.	______
Total	______	______	______	______	______	______	______	______

14. The following report shows the number of hours a month each assembler in a production line worked during the past six months. Find the total number of hours worked each month. Then find the 6-month total for each assembler as well as the total hours worked by all the assemblers in the 6-month period.

HOURS WORKED

WORKER	JANUARY	FEBRUARY	MARCH	APRIL	MAY	JUNE	TOTAL
Arnold	168	152	176	168	168	176	1008
Bernard	173	160	176	168	168	176	1021
Einhorn	168	160	176	173	168	186	1031
Grand	168	165	181	168	168	176	1016
Johnson	168	165	186	178	168	181	1046
Singer	168	160	168	164	168	176	1004
Victor	168	160	186	168	168	181	1031
Total	______	______	______	______	______	______	______

15. Find the number of tents sold each day, the total of each type sold during the week, and the total tents sold during the week.

DAILY SALES

TYPE OF TENT	MONDAY	TUESDAY	WEDNESDAY	THURSDAY	FRIDAY	TOTAL
Four-person lightweight tent	8	11	12	9	15	______
Two-person nylon tent	11	9	15	16	17	______
One-person pup tent	20	18	18	24	19	______
Six-person umbrella tent	1	-0-	-0-	1	-0-	______
Two-person tent with awning	3	4	3	5	2	______
Total	______	______	______	______	______	______

NAME DATE

SKILL BUILDER 4A

Increasing Speed in Addition

To improve speed and accuracy in addition, always make sure that numbers are written clearly and in uniform, straight columns and lines.

Large groups of numbers can be broken down into smaller groups. For example, break large groups into two or more subgroups, and add each of these subgroups. Then add the totals of the subgroups to find the grand total.

Add the numbers in these problems by finding subtotals at the places indicated and then by finding the overall total.

Ex.		1.		2.	
428		1,687		3,786	
645		765		4,508	
27		45		1,209	
156		4,525		7,459	
42	a. *1,298*	8,441	a. ______	6,663	a. ______
583		893		2,092	
897		757		5,698	
273		5,520		4,983	
6		43		3,678	
913	b. *2,672*	3,192	b. ______	1,954	b. ______
	c. *3,970*		c. ______		c. ______

3.		4.		5.	
$156.72		$ 6,095.76		$ 5,550.50	
85.34		1,980.75		12,465.83	
13.45		12,469.34		521.76	
873.54		45.08		4,590.21	
304.96	a. ______	2,460.55	a. ______	1,777.49	a. ______
45.98		422.33		22,432.65	
159.27		1,200.54		5,680.00	
484.53		4.38		34.91	
48.99		461.96		444.00	
417.46	b. ______	8,084.17	b. ______	4,872.37	b. ______
	c. ______		c. ______		c. ______

Another way to break down large groups of numbers is the **accountant's method of addition.** Each column of digits is added separately, and then the column totals are added. For example, to add 4,629 + 816 + 3,937 + 1,014, add the units first (9 + 6 + 7 + 4 = 26), the tens next (2 + 1 + 3 + 1 = 7), the hundreds next (6 + 8 + 9 + 0 = 23), and then the thousands (4 + 3 + 1 = 8). Finally, add the column totals.

Note that the column totals are staggered. When a column total is less than 10, put a zero in front of the number to ensure that the columns are aligned properly. This method of addition is particularly useful in work that is frequently interrupted.

```
  4,629
    816
  3,937
+ 1,014
     26
    07
   2 3
  8
 10,396
```


Add the numbers in these problems using the accountant's method of addition.

6.	7.	8.	9.
657	5,090	10,921	602
2,097	1,534	5,032	34,839
43	54	545	3,034
4,045	441	22,318	6,721
293	2,000	4,112	19
1,156	4,080	1,401	3,501

10. Bud's Discount House is open 24 hours, 7 days a week. Sales are tallied on the basis of three shifts—12 midnight to 8 a.m., 8 a.m. to 4 p.m., and 4 p.m. to 12 midnight. On the weekly sales report shown below, find the total for each department for each shift, the total of all sales for the day for each shift, the weekly total for each shift, and the day total of all sales for the week. The total of the Day Total row should equal the total of the Weekly Total column.

BUD'S DISCOUNT HOUSE WEEKLY SALES REPORT

DEPARTMENT	SUN.	MON.	TUES.	WED.	THURS.	FRI.	SAT.	WEEKLY TOTAL
Clothing	$ 453	$ 395	$ 404	$ 328	$ 420	$ 450	$ 615	______
Pharmacy	320	374	291	298	312	345	380	______
Hardware	95	114	105	83	118	154	165	______
Notions	192	183	156	133	94	190	125	______
Sports	108	95	82	211	106	174	115	______
Shift 1 Total								
Clothing	729	1,105	865	1,346	1,428	1,515	1,862	______
Pharmacy	540	495	611	502	1,003	908	1,432	______
Hardware	1,230	765	840	903	745	1,762	2,145	______
Notions	659	583	490	553	429	593	805	______
Sports	730	1,125	980	1,358	949	1,458	1,652	______
Shift 2 Total								
Clothing	564	435	446	358	475	497	712	______
Pharmacy	482	654	593	605	983	853	727	______
Hardware	1,154	839	1,157	720	835	1,156	1,341	______
Notions	634	602	545	524	487	627	790	______
Sports	874	972	1,382	892	869	821	945	______
Shift 3 Total								
Day Total								

NAME DATE

SKILL BUILDER 4B

Rounding Off Numbers and Estimating Answers

ROUNDING OFF NUMBERS **Rounding off** is replacing an actual figure or amount with an approximate figure. For example, sales of 19,883 items might be rounded off to "sales of around 20,000 items" for a verbal report. Money amounts are often rounded off to the nearest cent. A sales tax of $0.686 could be rounded off to $0.69.

To round off a number, first locate the place to which the number will be rounded. Then look at the digit to the right of this place. If this digit is between 5 and 9, increase the digit in the rounding place by 1. If this digit is between 1 and 4, leave the digit in the rounding place as is.

Example: Round off 5,627 to the tens place.

Solution: The digit in the tens place is 2. The digit to its right is 7. Since 7 is between 5 and 9, increase by 1 the digit in the tens place. The tens digit becomes 3 and the units digit is replaced with a zero.

5,627 rounds off to 5,630

Example: Round off 5,627 to the hundreds place.

Solution: The digit in the hundreds place is 6. The digit to its right is 2. Since 2 is between 1 and 4, leave the digit in the rounding place as is. Replace all digits to the right of the hundreds place with zeros.

5,627 rounds off to 5,600

When rounding off decimals, zeros are not added to the right of the rounded number. For example, 18.54 rounded off to the nearest tenth is 18.5; 45.668 rounded off to the nearest hundredth is 45.67.

Round off each number as indicated.

		ANSWERS
1.	553 to the nearest ten	1. ________
2.	8.605 to the nearest hundredth	2. ________
3.	$32.609 to the nearest dime	3. ________
4.	5,299.9 to the nearest thousand	4. ________
5.	17.839 to the nearest tenth	5. ________
6.	3.7056 to the nearest thousandth	6. ________
7.	23.92% to the nearest whole percent	7. ________
8.	59.49% to the nearest whole percent	8. ________
9.	763 to the nearest hundred	9. ________
10.	547 to the nearest thousand	10. ________
11.	16,572 to the nearest hundred	11. ________
12.	$46.219 to the nearest cent	12. ________
13.	0.05449 to the nearest tenth	13. ________
14.	23.7219 to the nearest hundredth	14. ________
15.	0.0776 to the nearest tenth	15. ________
16.	2.4986 to the nearest unit	16. ________
17.	17,605 to the nearest ten thousand	17. ________
18.	4.762% to the nearest tenth of a percent	18. ________

ESTIMATING ANSWERS IN ADDITION Estimating answers helps to uncover obvious errors in computations. Being able to estimate answers is especially important when using electronic calculators. By estimating answers, errors in totals, such as those caused by failure to enter a decimal point in the correct place, can be quickly recognized.

To estimate an answer to an addition problem, round off each number to its largest place. This will be the digit farthest to the left. Then add the rounded off numbers. The answer will be close to the actual answer.

Actual	*Estimate*	*Actual*	*Estimate*
322	300	2,529	3,000
576	600	1,432	1,000
349	300	770	800
105	100	4,200	4,000
1,352	1,300	8,931	8,800

Estimate the answer to each of the following problems by rounding off each number to its largest place and adding them. Then add the numbers to determine the actual totals. Compare your estimated answer with your actual answer to see if your actual answer is reasonable.

19.

ACTUAL	ESTIMATE
37	
61	
43	
89	
52	
46	
______	

20.

ACTUAL	ESTIMATE
88	
8	
52	
96	
12	
68	
______	

21.

ACTUAL	ESTIMATE
47	
62	
19	
39	
65	
22	
______	

22.

ACTUAL	ESTIMATE
737	
242	
495	
315	
389	
669	
______	

23.

ACTUAL	ESTIMATE
209	
454	
298	
549	
897	
242	
______	

24.

ACTUAL	ESTIMATE
785	
362	
411	
530	
647	
645	
______	

25.

ACTUAL	ESTIMATE
3,067	
4,198	
4,751	
2,009	
4,113	
4,851	
______	

26.

ACTUAL	ESTIMATE
4,381	
7,007	
3,436	
3,605	
1,651	
1,770	
______	

27.

ACTUAL	ESTIMATE
7,428	
3,664	
1,283	
4,245	
6,495	
2,629	
______	

NAME DATE

SKILL BUILDER 5A

Subtracting Numbers

In subtraction, each digit in the **subtrahend** is subtracted from the corresponding digit in the **minuend.** The result of the subtraction is called the **difference.** If a digit in the subtrahend is larger than the digit above it, it is necessary to borrow before subtracting. In the example below, 10 units are borrowed from the tens column and added to the units column.

$\overset{6}{\not7}\overset{1}{4}$	Minuend
−56	Subtrahend
18	Difference

CHECKING SUBTRACTION Check subtraction by adding the subtrahend to the difference; the sum should equal the minuend.

			CHECK	
7,870	Minuend		4,580	Subtrahend
−4,580	Subtrahend		+3,290	Difference
3,290	Difference		7,870	Minuend

Find the difference in each of these problems.

	a.	b.	c.	d.	e.	f.	g.
1.	97	42	40	61	73	89	65
	44	28	27	39	59	24	25
2.	561	402	852	820	818	211	604
	429	128	749	427	239	106	355

Find the difference in each problem. Check by adding the subtrahend to the difference.

	a.	b.	c.	d.	e.
3.	1,807	436	9,002	954	6,598
	643	278	4,928	643	2,693
4.	15,087	47,931	356,803	134,628	67,550
	13,258	28,853	58,999	99,999	32,536

5. **Net sales** is the difference between gross sales and sales returns. Determine the net sales for each day of the week for Essex Street Market.

ESSEX STREET MARKET

	SUN.	MON.	TUES.	WED.	THURS.	FRI.
Gross Sales	$10,943.	$8,678.	$7,586.	$8,840.	$9,624.	$12,955.
Sales Returns	217.	642.	258.	225.	195.	381.
Net Sales						

Business transactions are often recorded in a record called an **account.** An account resembles the letter *T.* The left side of the account is called the **debit** side; the right side of the account is called the **credit** side. To find how much is in the cash account, add all the debit amounts; then add all the credit amounts. The smaller number is subtracted from the larger number. If the total of the debit side is larger, the account has a **debit balance.** If the total of the credit side is larger, the account has a **credit balance.**

Cash	
160.00	56.25
2,650.50	643.90
65.45	85.00
492.11	234.75
745.73	1,019.90
4,113.79	

4,113.79
− 1,019.90
3,093.89 Debit balance

6. Add the debit and credit amounts in the accounts shown below. Subtract and determine whether the accounts have debit or credit balances.

Accounts Receivable	
5,678.90	790.00
790.00	2,678.90
1,434.08	434.08
53.25	500.00
2,000.00	53.25
194.34	
53.25	

Supplies	
150.00	50.00
65.00	6.75
93.56	12.80
29.04	
6.85	
42.09	

Equipment	
7,000.00	1,000.00
950.00	450.00
10,450.25	4,050.00
700.00	
3,450.50	
1,268.60	

Accounts Payable	
1,025.00	5,200.00
340.00	680.00
340.00	575.50
2,600.00	590.00
	3,090.75
	1,258.05

7. A cashier should make change in the fewest number of coins or bills possible. Use one dime, not two nickles. Use a $10 bill, not two $5 bills. Find the change for these purchases. Then select the correct coins and bills to make up the change.

	AMOUNT GIVEN IN PAYMENT	AMOUNT OF PURCHASE	AMOUNT OF CHANGE	1¢	5¢	10¢	25¢	$1	$5	$10	$20
Ex.	*$10.00*	*$ 2.58*	*$ 7.42*	*2*	*1*	*1*	*1*	*2*	*1*		
a.	5.00	1.49	________								
b.	7.00	6.43	________								
c.	20.00	5.04	________								
d.	15.00	12.51	________								
e.	1.00	.59	________								
f.	50.00	29.78	________								

NAME DATE

SKILL BUILDER 5B

Subtracting Horizontally and Estimating Answers

In horizontal subtraction, each digit in the subtrahend is subtracted from its counterpart in the minuend, units from units, tens from tens, and so on. The process is the same whether subtracting whole numbers or decimal fractions.

Subtraction, as well as addition, can be checked by computing both horizontally and vertically. The total of the horizontal minuends *less* the total of the horizontal subtrahends should equal the total of the horizontal differences.

ESTIMATING ANSWERS IN SUBTRACTION Answers to subtraction problems can be estimated by rounding off each number to its largest place—the digit farthest to the left—then subtracting the rounded off numbers. The answer will be close to the actual

Actual	*Estimate*	*Actual*	*Estimate*
29,689	30,000	39,872	40,000
− 12,271	− 10,000	− 6,819	− 7,000
17,418	20,000	33,053	30,000

Complete the following records and forms by subtracting horizontally.

1.

BIKE WORLD
WEEK OF APRIL 23, 19—

ITEM	BEGINNING	END	SALES
3-speed	40	12	______
10-speed	90	28	______
12-speed	125	35	______
20″ BMX	45	30	______
12″ RMX	35	23	______

2.

CHILDREN'S WEAR
MONTH OF AUGUST, 19—

ITEM	BEGINNING	END	SALES
Blouses	398	98	______
Dresses	435	124	______
Jackets	145	53	______
Jeans	503	218	______
Shirts	258	58	______
Shorts, Boys'	382	151	______
Shorts, Girls'	312	144	______
Skirts	482	224	______
Socks	505	132	______
Sweaters	165	76	______

3.

ACCOUNTS RECEIVABLE REPORT
SEPTEMBER 30, 19—

ACCOUNT NUMBER	BILLED	DISCOUNT ALLOWED	RECEIVED
115	$467.98	$18.72	______
125	190.23	3.80	______
155	102.45	3.07	______
165	93.25	0.93	______
185	303.46	9.10	______
195	88.72	0.89	______

4.

ACCOUNTS PAYABLE REPORT
SEPTEMBER 30, 19—

ACCOUNT NUMBER	AMOUNT DUE	AMOUNT PAID	BALANCE DUE
230	$1,456	$ 956	______
240	890	250	______
250	2,312	1,312	______
260	563	250	______
270	934	450	______
280	450	225	______

5. Ernest Enterprises maintains a check register in which the company records all checks that it writes to pay for invoices for merchandise that it has purchased. The amount of the check is the amount of the invoice less any cash discount. Complete the check register below and prove your computations.

CHECK REGISTER ERNEST ENTERPRISES JUNE 17, 19—			
CHECK NUMBER	AMOUNT OF INVOICE	CASH DISCOUNT	AMOUNT OF CHECK
577	$ 357.63	$10.73	______
578	1,982.75	99.14	______
579	145.90	2.92	______
580	55.67	–0–	______
581	598.50	29.93	______
582	346.38	10.39	______
583	28.25	–0–	______
584	481.09	19.24	______
Total	______	______	______

6. Complete the following inventory and prove your computations.

BIKE WORLD INVENTORY FOR WEEK ENDING APRIL 23, 19—			
ITEM	VALUE OF BEGINNING INVENTORY	AMOUNT OF SALES	VALUE OF INVENTORY ON HAND
3-speed	$ 3,399.60	$2,379.72	______
10-speed	8,099.10	5,579.38	______
12-speed	12,811.25	9,224.10	______
20″ BMX	3,143.25	1,047.75	______
12″ RMX	1,748.95	599.64	______
Total	______	______	______

7. Complete the following inventory and prove your computations.

SANDY'S SPORTSWEAR INC. INVENTORY FOR WEEK ENDING JULY 11, 19—			
ITEM	VALUE OF BEGINNING INVENTORY	AMOUNT OF SALES	VALUE OF INVENTORY ON HAND
Blouses	$2,358.09	$ 954.65	______
Halters	987.87	254.98	______
Jeans	3,459.22	1,040.75	______
Shoes, Canvas	1,009.45	550.34	______
Shoes, Leather	2,104.50	973.62	______
Shorts	1,985.02	654.82	______
Skirts	3,987.38	1,269.02	______
Tennis Dresses	1,753.72	703.45	______
Total	______	______	______

8. The following charts show the number of business starts and business failures for the years 19–6 and 19–7 in three regional areas. For each of the regions, determine the difference in business starts and failures.

BUSINESS STARTS	19–7	19–6	DIFFERENCE
Region A	4,964	5,455	491
Region B	19,877	21,708	1831
Region C	39,966	41,948	1982
Total	64 807	69,111	5304

BUSINESS FAILURES	19–7	19–6	DIFFERENCE
Region A	463	357	106
Region B	1,733	1,514	219
Region C	4,070	3,998	72
Total	5866	5869	397

Estimate the answer to each problem by rounding off each number to its largest place and then subtracting. Then find the actual difference.

9. **ACTUAL** **ESTIMATE**

  38,796
− 25,432

10. **ACTUAL** **ESTIMATE**

  36,329
− 5,124

11. **ACTUAL** **ESTIMATE**

  26,392
− 9,684

NAME DATE

SKILL BUILDER — Multiplying Numbers — 6A

MULTIPLYING WHOLE NUMBERS The number by which you multiply is the **multiplier,** the number being multiplied is the **multiplicand,** and the result of the computation is the **product.**

When the multiplier has two or more digits, the multiplicand is multiplied separately by each digit in the multiplier. These products are then added to find the final product. It is important to align the subproducts properly so that the correct answer will be obtained when the products are added.

```
   43  Multiplicand
 ×52  Multiplier
   86
 2 15
2,236  Product
```

MULTIPLYING DECIMALS Multiply decimals the same way whole numbers are multiplied. When the final product is obtained, place the decimal point so there are as many decimal places in the answer as there are in the multiplier and multiplicand combined. If there are not enough places in the product, add zeros to the *left* of the product to make up the required number of places. For example, multiply 5.089 × 0.005.

```
   5.089                      3 places
 ×0.005                      +3 places
0.025445   Add one zero. ← 6 places
```

Find the products and any totals.

1.
41 × 5 = ________
87 × 4 = ________
44 × 3 = ________
61 × 7 = ________
58 × 9 = ________
99 × 2 = ________
Total = ________

2.
359 × 6 = ________
7,412 × 9 = ________
432 × 3 = ________
1,546 × 7 = ________
435 × 8 = ________
3,452 × 4 = ________
Total = ________

3. 78 × 54

4. 856 × 32

5. 754 × 392

6. 8,065 × 44

7. 6,543 × 798

8. 842 × 53

9. 421 × 365

10. 5,384 × 779

11. 6,739 × 504

12. 9,126 × 867

Find the products. Round off final answers to the nearest hundredths.

13. 12.88 × 7

14. $34.92 × 5

15. $6.58 × 0.36

16. 16.928 × 1.007

ANSWERS

1. ________
2. ________
3. ________
4. ________
5. ________
6. ________
7. ________
8. ________
9. ________
10. ________
11. ________
12. ________
13. ________
14. ________
15. ________
16. ________

17. Compute the extensions on the invoice shown below by multiplying the quantity times the unit price. What is the total amount due?

GUTFELD HARDWARE COMPANY
234 Mandrake Avenue
Cleveland, OH 44118

To Bochner Home Supply Company
2654 Marston Road
Lyndhurst, OH 44124

Invoice Number 6308
Date May 24, 19--
Terms 2/10, n/30
Via Atlas Freight

	Quantity	Stock No.	Description	Unit Price	Amount
a.	24	ED-345	Electric drills-3/8 in.	$ 21.68	______
b.	54	SS-46S	Socket wrench set-standard	6.50	______
c.	18	SS-46M	Socket wrench set-metric	6.50	______
d.	144	LP-10	Locking plier-10 in.	1.50	______
e.	144	AW-8	Adjustable wrench-8 in.	2.28	______
				Total	______

18. Krazee Karl's Record Shop purchased 2,116 record albums, tapes, and compact discs from a bankrupt record store for $2.25 each. Karl sold them in his own shop at $7.89 each for the 1,587 albums, and $8.57 each for the 312 tapes. The rest, which were compact discs, were sold for $12.39 each.

a. How much did Krazee Karl receive from the sale of the 2,116 pieces?

b. What was the gross profit realized on this sale (total sales − cost of goods = gross profit)?

19. During a recent trip, Helen Betz purchased the following quantities of gasoline at the following prices: 14 gallons at $.979 a gallon; 18.6 gallons at $.918 a gallon; 19.5 gallons at $.877 a gallon; and 16.5 gallons at $.993 a gallon. How much did Helen spend for gasoline on her trip? Round off each purchase to the nearest cent, where necessary.

ANSWERS

17. ______

18. a. ______

b. ______

19. ______

NAME DATE

SKILL BUILDER 6B

Checking Multiplication and Estimating Answers

CHECKING THE ACCURACY OF MULTIPLICATION
One of the best ways to check the accuracy of multiplication is to divide the product by either the multiplier or the multiplicand. If the product is divided by the multiplicand, the answer should equal the multiplier. If the product is divided by the multiplier, the answer should equal the multiplicand. It is generally quicker to divide by the smaller of the two numbers.

```
   597          597             63
   ×63      63)37,611     597)37,611
  1 791        31 5           35 82
 35 82          6 11           1 791
 37,611         5 67           1 791
                 441
                 441
```

Another method of checking the accuracy of multiplication is to interchange the *factors* (the multiplier and the multiplicand) and multiply again. The product should be the same no matter what order the factors are multiplied.

```
    318       274
   ×274      ×318
   1 272     2 192
  22 26      2 74
  63 6      82 2
  87,132    87,132
```

Find the product for each of the following problems. Then check your answer by dividing the product by the multiplier. Show your work.

1.

a.	CHECK	b.	CHECK	c.	CHECK	d.	CHECK
95 × 23		358 × 74		716 × 48		430 × 852	

2.

a.	CHECK	b.	CHECK	c.	CHECK	d.	CHECK
3,725 × 612		8,008 × 907		4,500 × 425		4,045 × 222	

Find the product in each of the following problems. Then check your answer by interchanging the multiplier and the multiplicand. Show your work.

3. a.	CHECK	b.	CHECK	c.	CHECK	d.	CHECK
521		932		654		8,034	
424		283		29		419	

Shown below is a partial invoice. Check the invoice, and show the correct extensions and total.

4.

Quantity	Unit Price	Extension	ANSWERS
128 kg	$3.05 a kg	$390.40	
90 kg	1.19 a kg	101.70	
51 kg	0.51 a kg	26.01	
209 kg	0.81 a kg	179.29	
375 kg	1.10 a kg	412.50	
	Total	$1,109.90	

ESTIMATING ANSWERS IN MULTIPLICATION Answers to multiplication problems can be estimated by rounding off the multiplier and the multiplicand usually to the first digit and then multiplying the rounded off numbers. The answer obtained will be close to the actual answer. Do not round off single digit numbers.

Multiply 432 by 29.

Estimate	***Actual***
400	432
×30	×29
12,000	12,528

Multiply $9.95 by 38.

Estimate	***Actual***
$10	$9.95
×40	×38
$400	$378.10

When the second digit of a number is 5 or more, it is more accurate to round off to the second digit instead of the first.

Multiply 28,975 by 22.

Estimate	***Actual***
29,000	28,975
×20	×22
580,000	637,450

Multiply 31,244 by 276.

Estimate	***Actual***
30,000	31,244
×280	×276
8,400,000	8,623,344

Estimate the product. Then compute the actual answer.

5. a. ACTUAL	ESTIMATE	b. ACTUAL	ESTIMATE	c. ACTUAL	ESTIMATE	d. ACTUAL	ESTIMATE	e. ACTUAL	ESTIMATE
178		295		1,003		650		994	
8		19		32		21		101	

NAME DATE

SKILL BUILDER — Shortcuts in Multiplication — 7A

MULTIPLYING BY 10, 100, AND 1,000 To multiply by 10, move the decimal point of the multiplicand one place to the right. Add a zero if necessary.

495 × 10 = 495.0. or 4,950

To multiply by 100, move the decimal point two places to the right. Add zeros as necessary.

149.6 × 100 = 149.60. or 14,960

To multiply by 1,000, move the decimal point three places to the right. Add zeros as necessary.

150 × 1,000 = 150.000. or 150,000

MULTIPLYING BY MULTIPLES OF 10 To multiply by a *multiple* of 10 (for example, 40, 300, or 8,000), multiply by the first digit (4, 3, or 8). Then move the decimal point of the answer the required number of places to the right.

746 × 40 = ?
746 × 4 = 2,984
2,984 × 10 = 2,984.0. or 29,840

426 × 8,000 = ?
426 × 8 = 3,408
3,408 × 1,000 = 3,408.000. or 3,408,000

Use the shortcuts described above to find the product of each of the following problems. Then total each group.

			ANSWERS
1.	$ 875 × 10 =		1. ________
	36.85 × 100 =		________
	8.16 × 1,000 =		________
	62.50 × 400 =		________
	7.95 × 3,000 =		________
	679 × 90 =		________
	Total =		________
2.	49 × 50 =		2. ________
	127 × 80 =		________
	436 × 300 =		________
	62 × 9,000 =		________
	919 × 300 =		________
	1,585 × 500 =		________
	Total =		________
3.	327.68 × 400 =		3. ________
	560.11 × 60 =		________
	1.2222 × 4,000 =		________
	500 × 50 =		________
	616 × 700 =		________
	45 × 9,000 =		________
	Total =		________

ANSWERS

4. $3,857 × 50 = 4. ________
962 × 300 = ________
75 × 8,000 = ________
423 × 600 = ________
56 × 3,000 = ________
1,008 × 70 = ________
Total = ________

MULTIPLYING BY 25 OR BY A MULTIPLE OF 25 To multiply a number by 25, first multiply by 100, then divide by 4. For example, multiply 862 by 25.

862 × 100 = 862.00.
86,200 ÷ 4 = 21,550

To multiply by 50, multiply by 100 and divide by 2. For example, multiply 862 by 50.

862 × 100 = 862.00.
86,200 ÷ 2 = 43,100

To multiply by 125, first multiply by 1,000 and then divide by 8. For example, multiply 963 by 125.

963 × 1,000 = 963.000.
963,000 ÷ 8 = 120,375

To multiply by 250, multiply by 1,000 and divide by 4. To multiply by 500, multiply by 1,000 and divide by 2. To multiply by 750, multiply by 1,000 and divide by 4; multiply the result by 3.

Find the product for each of the following problems using the methods described above.

	a.	b.	c.
5.	465 × 50	785 × 25	924 × 25
6.	550 × 125	467 × 500	73 × 250
7.	$675.23 × 25	943 × 50	$150.50 × 250
8.	$179.45 × 50	$65.75 × 25	2,026 × 125
9.	$972.87 × 125	$45.38 × 500	4,658 × 250
10.	6,307 × 500	76 × 125	250 × 250
11.	375 × 50	1,280 × 125	470 × 500

ANSWERS

5. a. ________
b. ________
c. ________
6. a. ________
b. ________
c. ________
7. a. ________
b. ________
c. ________
8. a. ________
b. ________
c. ________
9. a. ________
b. ________
c. ________
10. a. ________
b. ________
c. ________
11. a. ________
b. ________
c. ________

NAME DATE

SKILL BUILDER 7B

Business Applications of Multiplication

1. Midtown News Service inventory shows the following record of newspapers sold last week. What is the total of each newspaper sold and the total wholesale cost to Midtown?

NEWSPAPER	DAILY SALES MON.	TUES.	WED.	THURS.	FRI.	SAT.	SUN.	TOTAL FOR WEEK	WHOLESALE UNIT PRICE	AMOUNT
A	350	375	320	360	370	280	–0–	______	$0.35	______
B	500	511	485	470	462	370	–0–	______	0.21	______
C	185	197	221	184	170	152	–0–	______	0.23	______
D	212	249	248	240	225	185	–0–	______	0.26	______
E	408	417	441	416	409	397	–0–	______	0.28	______
F	160	173	181	173	168	160	–0–	______	0.41	______
G	–0–	–0–	–0–	–0–	–0–	–0–	402	______	0.97	______
H	–0–	–0–	–0–	–0–	–0–	–0–	508	______	0.53	______
									Total cost	3056.17

2. Complete the invoice below.

Kaplan's Knits Inc.
1224 Crescent Street
San Francisco, CA 94111

To The Right Fit
3728 Harrison Street
Oakland, CA 94602

Invoice Number 385
Date May 10, 19--
Terms 2/10, n/30
Via PIE

	Quantity	Item	Unit Price	Amount
a.	16	Knit suits	$160.00	2560.00
b.	18	Polyester/cotton jumpsuits	52.00	936.00
c.	24	Knit tops	7.50	180.00
d.	40	Polyester knit shorts	9.75	390.00
e.	30 doz	Knee socks/doz	21.50	7740.00
f.	180	Polyester scarves	2.75	495.00
			Total	12 301.00

3. Complete the following weekly sales report. Use any multiplication shortcuts that may be applicable.

	BOY'S TOYS ELECTRONIC GAMES AND TOYS SALES WEEK OF FEBRUARY 27, 19—				
	QUANTITY	UNIT	ITEM	UNIT SELLING PRICE	TOTAL
a.	125	ea.	Super Video Game System	$79.99	________
b.	25	ea.	Radio Control Racer	99.99	________
c.	125	ea.	Game Software—Assorted	34.99	________
d.	1,000	pkg.	Batteries = C/D/9 volt	2.49	________
e.	50	ea.	Motorized Dinosaur	18.99	________
f.	500	ea.	Magnetic Board Games	3.99	________
				Total	________

4. Complete the following invoice.

	BUILDISCO BUILDERS P.O. BOX 8729—BELVIDERE, NJ 07823				
	ITEM NO.	QUANTITY	DESCRIPTION	PRICE/UNIT	EXTENSION
a.	24657	1 ea.	Hi-Performance Vac.	$ 69.99	________
b.	Stan10	7 ea.	Stain Brush—1 in.	2.59	________
c.	214SRSC	28 bx.	6 × 2¼ Sheet Rock Screws	3.82	________
d.	501-944	7 ea.	Exterior Door	169.99	________
e.	086-441	12 ea.	Window—3.2 × 4.5	152.60	________
f.	6-002-182	25 sht.	Plywood—⅝—CDX	10.79	________
g.	6-308-324	24 bdl.	Roof Shingles—Brown	6.49	________
h.	6-004-048	3 rls.	Roofing Felt—15 lb.	10.99	________
i.	6-114-02	50 lb.	Roofing Nails	.79	________
				Total	________

NAME DATE

SKILL BUILDER 8A

Dividing Numbers

DIVIDING WHOLE NUMBERS In division, the **dividend** is divided by the **divisor.** The result of the division process is the **quotient.** If the quotient is not a whole number, the fractional part can be expressed as a **remainder (R).** In the example below, the divisor (25) divides into the dividend (76) three times with a remainder of 1 (R1).

Quotient → 3, Remainder → R1

$$\begin{array}{r} 3\ \text{R}1 \\ \text{Divisor} \rightarrow 25\overline{)76} \leftarrow \text{Dividend} \\ -75 \\ \hline 1 \end{array}$$

To divide, estimate how many times the divisor will go into the dividend. In this example 25 can be divided into the dividend (76) three times. Write *3* in the quotient. Multiply the divisor by the estimate and subtract this product (75) from the dividend (76). The new dividend is 1. The answer could now be written as 3 R1, or the division process can be continued. To continue, bring down a zero from after the decimal point in the original dividend, making the new dividend *10.* 25 cannot be divided into 10, so put a zero in the quotient for this place. Bring down another zero, making the dividend 100. 25 goes into 100 four times. Write a 4 in the quotient. The answer is 3.04 and the remainder is zero.

$$\begin{array}{r} 3.04 \\ 25\overline{)76.00} \\ -75\ \downarrow\downarrow \\ \hline 1\ 00 \\ -1\ 00 \\ \hline 0 \end{array}$$

Find the quotient in each of the following problems. If the quotient is not a whole number, show what the remainder is.

1. $7\overline{)952}$
2. $4\overline{)1,684}$
3. $5\overline{)2,075}$
4. $3\overline{)2,474}$
5. $16\overline{)592}$
6. $43\overline{)9,419}$
7. $633\overline{)187,564}$
8. $458\overline{)219,158}$
9. $17\overline{)34,051}$
10. $18\overline{)63,018}$
11. $34\overline{)64,038}$
12. $123\overline{)426,441}$

ANSWERS

1. ________
2. ________
3. ________
4. ________
5. ________
6. ________
7. ________
8. ________
9. ________
10. ________
11. ________
12. ________

DIVIDING DECIMALS When a divisor is a decimal fraction or a mixed number, make the divisor a whole number by moving the decimal point as many places to the right as necessary. Also move the decimal point in the dividend the same number of places to the right, adding zeros if necessary. Then divide. For example, divide 62.01 by .018.

$$\text{Divisor} \quad .018.\overline{)62.010.} \quad \text{Dividend}, \qquad \text{Quotient} = 3{,}445.$$

When a number does not divide evenly, decide how far to carry out the computation. This depends on the degree of accuracy required. Money amounts are usually rounded off to the nearest cent. Divide one place further than the place required, and then round off to that place.

Round off the quotient to the nearest hundredth.

```
           407.611 → 407.61
.121.)49.321.000
      48 4
         921
         847
          74 0
          72 6
           1 40
           1 21
             190
             121
              69R
```

Find the quotient in each problem. Round off your answers to the nearest ten thousandth (unless the computation results in a zero remainder).

13. $2.6\overline{)4{,}596.8}$

14. $5.02\overline{)1{,}562}$

15. $13\overline{)3{,}445.27}$

16. $.083\overline{)175.29}$

17. $31.2\overline{)547}$

18. $109\overline{)65.952}$

ANSWERS

13. ________

14. ________

15. ________

16. ________

17. ________

18. ________

NAME DATE

SKILL BUILDER 8B

Checking Division and Estimating Answers

To check the accuracy of a division computation, multiply the divisor by the quotient and add any remainder. The result should equal the dividend.

(Divisor × Quotient) + Remainder = Dividend

```
   149          CHECK
23)3,427          149
   2 3           ×23
   1 12           447
     92         2 98
    207         3,427
    207
```

```
    99 R12      CHECK
26)2,586           99
   2 34           ×26
    246           594
    234          1 98
     12R         2 574
                  +12
                 2,586
```

Find the quotient in each problem, and indicate what the remainder is, if any. Check your answers by the method shown above. Show the details of your work.

1. 62)3,658 CHECK

2. 38)5,780 CHECK

3. 84)9,660 CHECK

4. 75)22,726 CHECK

5. 5)251,530 CHECK

6. 42)11,258 CHECK

ANSWERS

1. ____________
2. ____________
3. ____________
4. ____________
5. ____________
6. ____________

The same method of checking can be used whenever the quotient is a mixed decimal fraction. However, if the quotient has been rounded off, the product of the quotient multiplied by the divisor will not equal the dividend exactly.

```
      439.19791
96)42,163.00000
```

439.19791 × 96 = 42,162.999

439.1979 × 96 = 42,162.998

439.198 × 96 = 42,163.008

439.2 × 96 = 42,163.2

439 × 96 = 42,144

Find the quotient in each problem. Round off your answer to the nearest hundredth. Check your answer by multiplying the rounded quotient by the divisor.

7. 48)3,985 CHECK

8. 77)15,864 CHECK

9. 36)1,730 CHECK

ANSWERS

7. ________

8. ________

9. ________

ESTIMATING ANSWERS IN DIVISION Answers to division problems can be estimated by rounding off the divisor and the dividend usually to the first digit. If the divisor is a single-digit number, it is not necessary to round off that number.

Actual	*Estimate*
48)6,192 = 129	50)6,000 = 120
8)1,242.00 = 155.25	8)1,000 = 125

When the second digit of a number is 5 or more, it's more accurate to round off to the second digit instead of the first.

Actual	*Estimate*
152)17,784 = 117	150)18,000 = 120

Estimate the answers. Then find the actual answers. Show the details of your work. Round off to the nearest hundredth.

10. ACTUAL 42)8,254 ESTIMATE

11. ACTUAL 28)9,256 ESTIMATE

12. ACTUAL 398)15,904 ESTIMATE

13. ACTUAL 91)2,650 ESTIMATE

14. ACTUAL 68)4,256 ESTIMATE

15. ACTUAL 29)6,822 ESTIMATE

NAME DATE

SKILL BUILDER 9A

Using Shortcuts in Division

DIVIDING BY 10, 100, OR 1,000 To divide by 10, move the decimal point one place to the left. (The decimal point in a whole number is always to the right of the last digit.)

1,568 ÷ 10 = 156.8. → 156.8

47.693 ÷ 10 = 4.7.693 → 4.7693

To divide by 100, move the decimal point two places to the left. To divide by 1,000, move the decimal point three places to the left. If necessary, add zeros to the left of the dividend.

4,657.2 ÷ 100 = 46.57.2 → 46.572

11.5894 ÷ 1,000 = 0.011.5894 → 0.0115894

If the divisor is a multiple of 10, such as 40, 700, or 3,000, first move the decimal point in the dividend as many places to the left as there are zeros in the divisor. Then divide the resulting number by the non-zero digit (in this case, 4, 7, or 3) to find the quotient.

1,850 ÷ 40	96.3 ÷ 3,000
1,850 ÷ 10 = 185.0.	96.3 ÷ 1,000 = 0.096.3
185 ÷ 4 = 46.25	0.0963 ÷ 3 = 0.0321

For each problem, find the quotients and the total. Divide as far as possible. Use the shortcut methods described above, and show only your answers. Be sure to align the quotients so the numbers can be added.

1. 854 ÷ 1,000 = ________

1,467 ÷ 10 = ________

42,345 ÷ 100 = ________

8,640 ÷ 500 = ________

762 ÷ 40 = ________

1,000 ÷ 10 = ________

10,000 ÷ 100 = ________

Total = ________

2. 19,450 ÷ 4,000 = ________

58,209 ÷ 3,000 = ________

7,412 ÷ 800 = ________

164 ÷ 400 = ________

882 ÷ 700 = ________

6,500 ÷ 1,000 = ________

329 ÷ 10 = ________

Total = ________

3. $757.42	÷	80	=	$__________
96.844	÷	400	=	__________
357.64	÷	2,000	=	__________
327.70	÷	500	=	__________
900.00	÷	10	=	__________
65.92	÷	4,000	=	__________
947.65	÷	100	=	__________
		Total	=	$__________

DIVIDING BY 25 OR A MULTIPLE OF 25 To divide by 25, first divide by 100. Then multiply the result by 4. This works because dividing by 25 gives a quotient four times larger than dividing by 100. Divide 429 by 25.

429 ÷ 100 = 4.29.   4.29 × 4 = 17.16

To divide by 50, first divide by 100. Then multiply the result by 2. Divide 357 by 50.

357 ÷ 100 = 3.57.   3.57 × 2 = 7.14

To divide by 125, first divide by 1,000. Then multiply the result by 8. Divide $6,160 by 125.

$6,160 ÷ 1,000 = $6.160. $6.16 × 8 = $49.28

To divide by 250, first divide by 1,000. Then multiply the result by 4. To divide by 500, first divide by 1,000. Then multiply the result by 2.

Find the quotient in each of the following problems. Use the shortcut methods, and show your work. For money amounts, round off your final answers to the nearest cent where necessary.

4. 3,260 ÷ 25   **5.** $1,729.50 ÷ 50   **6.** 8,475 ÷ 250

7. $6,750 ÷ 125   **8.** $418.90 ÷ 125   **9.** $202.50 ÷ 25

10. 4,650 ÷ 125   **11.** 217.6 ÷ 250   **12.** 9,850 ÷ 500

13. 13,500 ÷ 25   **14.** 33,750 ÷ 500   **15.** 847.5 ÷ 50

16. $17,295 ÷ 250   **17.** $21,760 ÷ 125   **18.** 4,930 ÷ 500

ANSWERS

4. __________
5. __________
6. __________
7. __________
8. __________
9. __________
10. __________
11. __________
12. __________
13. __________
14. __________
15. __________
16. __________
17. __________
18. __________

Many products are priced and sold in units of 100 or 1,000. C is the abbreviation for 100 units. A hundredweight, or 100 pounds, is abbreviated **cwt.** M is the abbreviation for 1,000 units. A thousand board-feet of lumber would be abbreviated MB or MBF.

550 envelopes @ \$2.50 a C = 5.5 × \$2.50 = \$13.75

5,250 board feet lumber @ \$27 a MBF = 5.25 × \$27
= \$141.75

650 pounds sugar @ \$33.50 a cwt = 6.5 × \$33.50
= \$217.75

8,650 kilograms potash @ \$159 for 1,000 kg
= 8.65 × \$159
= \$1,375.35

Dozen = dz = 12 pieces
Gross = gr = 144 pieces
720 seed packs @ \$57.60/gr
720 ÷ 144 = 5 gr × \$57.60 = \$288.00

Complete the extensions on each of the following invoices. Round off to the nearest cent, where necessary.

19.

Gladeau Garden Supply
212 State Highway 30
Hohokus, New Jersey 07423

Invoice No. 11857

To The Green Thumb
1123 East End Road
Weehawken, NJ 07087

Date March 3, 19--
Terms C.O.D.
Via Pickup

	Quantity	Item	Unit Price	Amount
a.	7,900 kg	# 18-216 Weed block	\$ 909/1,000 kg	________
b.	1,158 lbs	# 18-128 Green seed	133.33/cwt	________
c.	832 bags	# 18-861 Peat grow-40 lb	80.00/C bags	________
d.	850 yards	# 18-887 Burlap	970/M yards	________
			Total	________

20.

Milton Paper Supply
843 Ridgedale Avenue
Cedar Knolls, PA 18350

Invoice No. 12289

To Rainbow Caterers
4298 Mt Pleasant Avenue
Livingwell, NJ 07793

Date May 1, 19--
Terms Net
Via Delivered

	Item No.	Quantity	Description	Price/Unit	Extension
a.	11-852	10 M	Napkins - economy	\$3.708/M	________
b.	41-725	250 C	Plates - 5 inch	2.875/C	________
c.	41-730	110 C	Plates - 10 inch	5.21/C	________
d.	58-0710	420 dz	Cutlery sets	21.60/gr	________
e.	29-365	5 1	Liquid Kleen concentrate	2.89/1	________
				Total	________

21.

M. Switzer and Son Inc.
2015 Jersey Avenue • Euclid, OH 44120

To Euclid Art Supplies
4285 Race Street
Euclid, OH 44120

Invoice Number 1285
Date February 25, 19--
Terms Net
Via Picked up

	Quantity	Item	Unit Price	Amount
a.	15 rolls	Nu-Felt - 50 yards/roll	$ 45.00/c yards	
b.	6 doz	Watercolor sets	338.40/gr	
c.	25,000 shts	Kraft paper-assorted colors	19.50/M	
d.	49.5 kg	Sculpt-clay	418./100 kg	
e.	629 sq ft	Canvas board-assorted sizes	369./M sq ft	
			Total	

22.

M. Switzer and Son Inc.
2015 Jersey Avenue • Euclid, OH 44120

To Hopewell Enterprises
853 Spinning Road
Dayton, Ohio 45431

Invoice Number 1292
Date April 12, 19--
Terms C.O.D.
Via Lee's Express

	Quantity	Item	Unit Price	Amount
a.	48 cases	Duplicating paper-5M shts/cse	$ 9.78/M sheets	
b.	6 gr	Ball point pens	1.29/dz.	
c.	4 cases	Toner - 10 kg/case	15.98/kg	
d.	6 dozen	Mylar ribbon cartridges	228.96/gr	
e.	11.5 M	Envelopes - #10	4.85/C	
			Total	

23. Complete the invoice below.

Seoul Electronics International
Mount Olive Foreign Trade Zone

To Sight and Sound
1128 Bay Street
Seattle, WA 08593

Invoice No. 11840
Date April 17, 19--
Terms 5/10, 2/30, n/45

	Item	Quantity	Description	Unit Price	Amount
a.	VR2400/6267	38	VCR - Remote/Digital	$ 113.43	
b.	DX610/6312	60	Compact Disc Player	56.99	
c.	8200/3078	75	Digital Car Stereo	56.98	
d.	81/TRI6	150	Speaker - Triaxial	17.01	
e.	1955/3108	20	Color TV - Remote 19 in.	170.43	
f.	SCA-630	4	200 Watt Stereo System	455.43	
				Sub-Total	
				Freight	
				Total	

NAME DATE

SKILL BUILDER 9B

Computing Averages

An **average** is found by dividing the sum of a set of numbers by the number of items in the set. This kind of average is called a mean average. For example, during a three-year period, a sales representative earned $28,900; $32,450; and $38,526. Find the average annual income for this period.

$28,900
32,450
38,526
$99,876 total three-year income

$99,876 ÷ 3 = $33,292 average annual income

ANSWERS

1. ________
2. ________
3. a. ________
   b. ________
4. a. ________
   b. ________

1. During this year's United Campaign, 112 communities in Morris County contributed a total of $4,974,144. What was the average contribution per community?

2. Four sales representatives employed by Randolph Realty Associates earned $4,220; $2,965; $3,763; and $5,175 during the past month. What was the average of their monthly earnings?

3. Marge Pineros is a sales representative with Randolph Realty Associates. For the past 12 months, her earnings were $3,363; $3,695; $3,215; $4,150; $2,915; $4,197; $3,496; $3,751; $3,215; $3,935; $3,202; and $3,525.

a. What were her total earnings for the year?

b. What were her average monthly earnings to the nearest cent?

4. The nine sales representatives for Bledsoe Products had expense accounts for the past three months as follows: $1,128; $1,374; $801; $1,506; $1,251; $888; $1,029; $1,311; and $1,533.

a. What was the average expense account for the three month period?

b. What was the average monthly expense account?

ANSWERS

5. a. ______

b. ______

6. ______

7. ______

8. ______

9. ______

5. Marge Chandler uses her car for business. For the past year, she drove the following mileage.

QUARTER	MILES	GALLONS OF GAS USED	TOTAL COST
Jan.–Mar.	1,856	111	206016
Apr.–June	3,035	196	594860
July–Sept.	3,774	240	905760
Oct.–Dec.	2,870	163	467810
Total	11535	710	2,17,4446

a. What was her average mileage for a gallon of gas? Round off your answer to the nearest hundredth.
b. What was the average price she paid for a gallon? Round off your answer to the nearest cent.

6. A jeweler sold the following numbers of rings each week during a recent month: 93, 84, 90, 77. What was the average number of rings sold a week?

7. The weekly commissions for Greg Restik, a furniture salesperson, for the past four weeks were $1,000, $850, $1,200, and $900. What was his average amount of commissions a week?

8. Joan Simmons, a produce auctioneer, took a total of 3,000 bags of potatoes to auction. Of the 3,000 bags, 40 bags were spoiled and were dumped prior to the sale. 960 bags were sold for $6.75 per bag; 1,100 bags for $6.25 per bag; 500 bags for $7.15 per bag; and the remainder for $7.05 per bag. What was the average price per bag?

9. Long's Lilies bought 3,500 planters for $3,500 at a bankruptcy auction. It sold 1,850 planters for $2.70 each, and 1,000 for $2.85 each. How much would Long's Lilies have to sell the balance for to the nearest cent in order to realize an average selling price of $3 a planter?

NAME DATE

SKILL BUILDER — Renaming Fractions — 10A

A fraction is a number written in this form: $\frac{2}{3}$. The number above the line is the **numerator;** the number below the line is the **denominator.** The numerator and denominator are the **terms** of the fraction. A fraction whose numerator is smaller than its denominator is a **proper fraction** and always has a value of less than 1.

RENAMING FRACTIONS TO LOWEST TERMS To rename a fraction in lower terms, find a number that is contained an even number of times in both the numerator and the denominator. Dividing both the numerator and the denominator by this number will result in a fraction equal in value to the original fraction but made up of smaller numbers. When no number other than 1 will divide evenly into both terms, a fraction is said to be **in lowest terms.** Rename $\frac{12}{28}$ in lowest terms. Since both 12 and 28 are divisible by 2, it is possible to either divide successively by 2 until lowest terms are reached, or to use some multiple of 2 to obtain the same results.

$$\frac{12}{28} = \frac{12 \div 2}{28 \div 2} = \frac{6}{14} = \frac{6 \div 2}{14 \div 2} = \frac{3}{7}$$

$$\frac{12}{28} = \frac{12 \div 4}{28 \div 4} = \frac{3}{7}$$

Rename the following fractions to lowest terms.

1. $\frac{6}{16} =$
2. $\frac{15}{35} =$
3. $\frac{16}{24} =$
4. $\frac{27}{81} =$
5. $\frac{18}{72} =$
6. $\frac{9}{45} =$
7. $\frac{14}{20} =$
8. $\frac{36}{42} =$
9. $\frac{27}{33} =$
10. $\frac{18}{27} =$
11. $\frac{14}{84} =$
12. $\frac{21}{42} =$
13. $\frac{14}{42} =$
14. $\frac{26}{39} =$
15. $\frac{15}{25} =$
16. $\frac{28}{40} =$
17. $\frac{17}{51} =$
18. $\frac{28}{36} =$

ANSWERS

1. ________
2. ________
3. ________
4. ________
5. ________
6. ________
7. ________
8. ________
9. ________
10. ________
11. ________
12. ________
13. ________
14. ________
15. ________
16. ________
17. ________
18. ________

RENAMING FRACTIONS TO HIGHER TERMS When a fraction must be renamed to an equivalent fraction with a larger denominator, divide the new denominator (the larger term) by the denominator of the fraction being renamed. Use this quotient to multiply both the numerator and denominator of the fraction to be renamed. For example, rename $\frac{2}{15}$ in 60ths.

$$60 \div 15 = 4$$

$$\frac{2}{15} = \frac{2 \times 4}{15 \times 4} = \frac{8}{60}$$

Because $\frac{4}{4} = 1$, multiplying or dividing any number by such a fraction does not change the real value of the fraction because it is actually multiplying or dividing by 1.

Rename the following fractions to the higher terms indicated.

19. $\frac{2}{3}$ to 27ths **20.** $\frac{3}{8}$ to 32nds **21.** $\frac{2}{5}$ to 40ths **22.** $\frac{11}{12}$ to 36ths

23. $\frac{4}{32}$ to 96ths **24.** $\frac{5}{18}$ to 72nds **25.** $\frac{3}{7}$ to 56ths **26.** $\frac{4}{15}$ to 90ths

ANSWERS

19. ________
20. ________
21. ________
22. ________
23. ________
24. ________
25. ________
26. ________

RENAMING IMPROPER FRACTIONS AS WHOLE OR MIXED NUMBERS A fraction whose numerator is equal to or greater than its denominator is an **improper fraction.** A **mixed number** is a combination of a whole number and a fraction. To rename an improper fraction as a mixed number, divide the denominator into the numerator. Rename any remainder to its lowest terms.

$$\frac{30}{4} = 7\frac{2}{4} = 7\frac{1}{2}$$

RENAMING WHOLE NUMBERS AS IMPROPER FRACTIONS To rename a whole number as a fraction, simply write the whole number as the numerator with a denominator of 1. For example, rename 3 and 15 as fractions.

$$3 = \frac{3}{1} \qquad 15 = \frac{15}{1}$$

Rename the following improper fractions as whole or mixed numbers.

27. $\frac{12}{10} =$ **28.** $\frac{9}{9} =$ **29.** $\frac{58}{26} =$

30. $\frac{117}{20} =$ **31.** $\frac{51}{12} =$ **32.** $\frac{46}{14} =$

ANSWERS

27. ________
28. ________
29. ________
30. ________
31. ________
32. ________

Rename these whole numbers as improper fractions.

ANSWERS

33. 75 = 34. 13 = 35. 4 = 36. 166 = 37. 1 =

33. ________
34. ________
35. ________
36. ________
37. ________

RENAMING MIXED NUMBERS AS IMPROPER FRACTIONS To rename a mixed number as an improper fraction, multiply the whole number by the denominator in the fraction, and add the numerator of the fraction to this product. Place this new numerator over the denominator of the mixed number fraction. For example, rename $7\frac{2}{5}$ as an improper fraction.

$7 \times 5 = 35 \qquad 35 + 2 = 37 \qquad 7\frac{2}{5} = \frac{37}{5}$

RENAMING FRACTIONS AS DECIMAL FRACTIONS To rename a proper fraction as a decimal fraction, divide the numerator by the denominator. When the division ends in a run-on number, either round off the run-on number or express it as a common fraction. For example, rename $\frac{3}{8}$ and $\frac{1}{6}$ as decimal fractions.

$8\overline{)3.000} = 0.375 \qquad 6\overline{)1.0000} = 0.1666$ or 0.167 or $0.16\frac{2}{3}$

Rename the following mixed numbers as improper fractions.

ANSWERS

38. $5\frac{4}{6}$ 39. $16\frac{2}{3}$ 40. $3\frac{5}{9}$

41. $3\frac{5}{7}$ 42. $4\frac{5}{11}$ 43. $12\frac{3}{5}$

38. ________
39. ________
40. ________
41. ________
42. ________
43. ________
44. ________
45. ________
46. ________
47. ________

Rename the following fractions as decimal fractions. Round off any run-on numbers to the third decimal place.

44. $\frac{5}{16}$ 45. $\frac{4}{32}$ 46. $\frac{1}{9}$ 47. $\frac{28}{64}$

RENAMING DECIMAL FRACTIONS AS PROPER FRACTIONS To rename a decimal fraction as a proper fraction, write the decimal fraction as the numerator (without a decimal point) over a denominator of 1, plus as many zeros as there are places to the right of the decimal point. For example, rename 0.56 and $0.5\frac{1}{2}$ as proper fractions in lowest terms.

$$0.56 = \frac{56}{100} = \frac{56 \div 4}{100 \div 4} = \frac{14}{25}$$

$$0.5\tfrac{1}{2} = 0.55 = \frac{55}{100} = \frac{55 \div 5}{100 \div 5} = \frac{11}{20}$$

Rename the following decimal fractions as proper fractions. Rename the answers in lowest terms.

48. 0.48 **49.** 0.625 **50.** 0.375

51. $0.16\frac{1}{4}$ **52.** $0.22\frac{2}{5}$ **53.** $0.11\frac{1}{9}$

54. 0.1875 **55.** 0.15625 **56.** 1.80

57. 2.125 **58.** $3.366\frac{2}{3}$ **59.** $0.2727\frac{3}{11}$

ANSWERS

48. ____________

49. ____________

50. ____________

51. ____________

52. ____________

53. ____________

54. ____________

55. ____________

56. ____________

57. ____________

58. ____________

59. ____________

NAME DATE

SKILL BUILDER 10B

Finding the Lowest Common Denominator

When a group of fractions are to be added or subtracted, all the fractions must have the same denominator. If the denominators are not the same, the fractions must be renamed as fractions with the same denominator. The smallest denominator which is common to all the fractions—the lowest common denominator (l.c.d.)—should be used. Three ways to do this are shown in this skill builder.

1. *Inspection or Trial.* 12 is the smallest denominator common to all 3 fractions.

$$\frac{3}{4} = \frac{9}{12}$$
$$\frac{2}{3} = \frac{8}{12}$$
$$+\frac{5}{6} = +\frac{10}{12}$$
$$\frac{27}{12} = 2\tfrac{3}{12} = 2\tfrac{1}{4}$$

2. *Product of the Denominators.* Multiplying the denominators will produce a common denominator, but it will not necessarily be the smallest one. For example, using the denominators in the inspection method at left, $4 \times 3 \times 6$ would produce a common denominator of 72, which is not the lowest common denominator. Another method is to select the largest denominator from among the group of fractions. Starting with the smallest, multiply each of the other denominators by the largest one until the lowest denominator is found which is evenly divisible by each of the other denominators. For example, in the problem $\frac{2}{9} + \frac{1}{2} + \frac{1}{4} + \frac{1}{8}$, 9 is the largest denominator.

$9 \times 2 = 18 \leftarrow$ not divisible by 8

$9 \times 4 = 36 \leftarrow$ not divisible by 8

$9 \times 8 = 72 \leftarrow$ lowest common denominator

If the product of two of the denominators does not result in a lowest common denominator, it may be necessary to multiply by additional factors until a product is found which is evenly divisible by all of the original denominators.

Find the lowest common denominator for the following groups of fractions, using one of the above methods.

1. $\frac{1}{2} + \frac{2}{3} + \frac{3}{4} + \frac{1}{6}$

2. $\frac{1}{2} + \frac{5}{8} + \frac{7}{18} + \frac{3}{4}$

3. $\frac{2}{3} + \frac{1}{4} + \frac{4}{15} + \frac{7}{8}$

4. $\frac{1}{9} + \frac{3}{8} + \frac{5}{12} + \frac{1}{4}$

5. $\frac{3}{4} + \frac{3}{16} + \frac{2}{3} + \frac{5}{8}$

6. $\frac{3}{5} + \frac{4}{15} + \frac{11}{12} + \frac{2}{3}$

ANSWERS

1. ________
2. ________
3. ________
4. ________
5. ________
6. ________

ANSWERS

7. $\frac{1}{3} + \frac{5}{21} + \frac{4}{9} + \frac{1}{15}$

8. $\frac{7}{12} + \frac{2}{3} + \frac{1}{8} + \frac{3}{5}$

7. ________

8. ________

If the lowest common denominator is not obvious by inspection or requires extensive multiplication to use the second method, use the prime number method.

3. *Prime Numbers.* A **prime number** is one which is divisible only by 1 and itself. 2, 3, 5, 7, 11, 13, and 17 are examples of prime numbers. To determine the lowest common denominator by this method, do the following steps.

a. List all the denominators.

b. Beginning with the lowest prime number other than 1 as the divisor, divide the denominators and bring down the results.

c. Continue dividing the results by prime numbers until all the results are reduced to 1.

d. Find the product of all the prime numbers used. The product is the lowest common denominator.

$$\frac{3}{8} + \frac{1}{7} + \frac{7}{10} + \frac{5}{16} + \frac{2}{5}$$

a	2	8	7	10	16	5
b	2	4	7	5	8	5
c	2	2	7	5	4	5
	2	1	7	5	2	5
	5	1	7	5	1	5
	7	1	7	1	1	1
		1	1	1	1	1

d $2 \times 2 \times 2 \times 2 \times 5 \times 7 = 560$
lowest common denominator

Find the lowest common denominator for the following groups of fractions.

ANSWERS

9. $\frac{2}{3} + \frac{1}{15} + \frac{3}{4} + \frac{5}{8} + \frac{1}{2}$

10. $\frac{1}{2} + \frac{5}{6} + \frac{1}{7} + \frac{1}{4} + \frac{1}{3}$

11. $\frac{5}{12} + \frac{1}{3} + \frac{1}{2} + \frac{5}{9} + \frac{1}{7}$

12. $\frac{3}{5} + \frac{1}{4} + \frac{1}{11} + \frac{7}{15} + \frac{1}{8}$

13. $\frac{1}{6} + \frac{7}{30} + \frac{3}{16} + \frac{5}{32} + \frac{3}{8}$

14. $\frac{3}{13} + \frac{5}{9} + \frac{7}{12} + \frac{1}{8} + \frac{11}{20}$

9. ________

10. ________

11. ________

12. ________

13. ________

14. ________

NAME DATE

SKILL BUILDER 11A

Adding Common Fractions and Mixed Numbers

Fractions can be added only when they have like denominators. The total of the numerators of the addends is the numerator of the sum. The common denominator of the addends becomes the denominator of the sum. Rename the fraction in lowest terms if necessary.

$$\begin{array}{r} \frac{3}{19} \\ +\frac{7}{19} \\ \hline \frac{10}{19} \end{array} \qquad \begin{array}{r} \frac{7}{24} \\ +\frac{11}{24} \\ \hline \frac{18}{24} \end{array} = \frac{3}{4} \qquad \begin{array}{r} \frac{4}{5} \\ +\frac{3}{5} \\ \hline \frac{7}{5} \end{array} = 1\frac{2}{5}$$

When the denominators are not all the same, the lowest common denominator must be found; all fractions must then be renamed in like terms. For example, add $27\frac{3}{8} + 13\frac{5}{16} + 3\frac{1}{3} + 2\frac{5}{6}$. The lowest common denominator is 48. The whole numbers and fractions are added separately; then they are combined.

$$\begin{array}{rcl} 27\frac{3}{8} & = & 27\frac{18}{48} \\ 13\frac{5}{16} & = & 13\frac{15}{48} \\ 3\frac{1}{3} & = & 3\frac{16}{48} \\ +2\frac{5}{6} & = & 2\frac{40}{48} \\ \hline & & 45\frac{89}{48} = 45 + 1\frac{41}{48} = 46\frac{41}{48} \end{array}$$

Add the following groups of fractions. Rename the answers in lowest terms.

1. $2\frac{1}{4}$, $4\frac{3}{8}$, $3\frac{11}{32}$, $2\frac{1}{2}$, $3\frac{1}{16}$

2. $7\frac{7}{18}$, $3\frac{5}{6}$, $3\frac{1}{3}$, $5\frac{5}{12}$, $2\frac{5}{9}$

3. $16\frac{1}{8}$, $9\frac{2}{5}$, $2\frac{7}{15}$, $3\frac{7}{9}$, $1\frac{1}{16}$

4. $4\frac{3}{5}$, $2\frac{3}{7}$, $5\frac{3}{4}$, $2\frac{3}{14}$, $1\frac{1}{8}$

5. $4\frac{3}{8}$, $3\frac{2}{3}$, $3\frac{7}{12}$, $2\frac{4}{9}$, $3\frac{1}{2}$

6. $5\frac{7}{30}$, $2\frac{1}{11}$, $3\frac{5}{6}$, $2\frac{2}{3}$, $6\frac{2}{5}$

ANSWERS

1. ____________
2. ____________
3. ____________
4. ____________
5. ____________
6. ____________

7.

$4\frac{1}{4}$
$2\frac{1}{3}$
$3\frac{1}{3}$
$9\frac{3}{4}$
$1\frac{1}{8}$

8.

$12\frac{1}{6}$
$9\frac{2}{3}$
$5\frac{5}{6}$
$11\frac{5}{24}$
$10\frac{1}{8}$

9.

$8\frac{5}{8}$
$19\frac{2}{5}$
$6\frac{2}{9}$
$23\frac{5}{12}$
$10\frac{1}{4}$

ANSWERS

7. ________
8. ________
9. ________

Fractions can also be added by using the decimal equivalent. A fraction is expressed as its decimal equivalent by dividing the denominator into the numerator.

$\frac{1}{2}$ $2\overline{)1.0}$ = 0.5	$\frac{1}{3}$ $3\overline{)1.0000}$ = 0.3333	$\frac{5}{8}$ $8\overline{)5.000}$ = 0.625
$\frac{3}{4}$ $4\overline{)3.00}$ = 0.75	$\frac{4}{5}$ $5\overline{)4.0}$ = 0.8	$\frac{1}{16}$ $16\overline{)1.0000}$ = 0.0625

Sometimes numbers will be in a mixed form, containing both a decimal fraction and a common fraction. When this occurs, express all the numbers as either decimal fractions or as common fractions before proceeding with the addition.

Add as Fractions			*Add as Decimals*
$6\frac{1}{2}$	=	$6\frac{8}{16}$	6.5000
$3\frac{5}{8}$	=	$3\frac{10}{16}$	3.6250
$4\frac{1}{16}$	=	$4\frac{1}{16}$	4.0625
$+2\frac{3}{4}$	=	$2\frac{12}{16}$	+2.7500
		$15\frac{31}{16} = 16\frac{15}{16}$	16.9375

Note: 0.9375 is equivalent to $\frac{15}{16}$

$0.37\frac{1}{2} = 0.3750$
$0.42\frac{1}{4} = 0.4225$
$\frac{5}{8} = 0.6250$
$+0.48\frac{2}{3} = 0.4867$
1.9092

Add the following groups of numbers by renaming all addends as decimal fractions. Round off to 5 decimal places, where necessary.

10.

$\frac{5}{16}$
$0.37\frac{1}{2}$
$0.15\frac{1}{8}$
$\frac{1}{32}$

11.

$7.16\frac{3}{4}$
$6.25\frac{2}{5}$
$8.9\frac{5}{6}$
$6.02\frac{1}{4}$

12.

$0.87\frac{1}{2}$
$6.7\frac{1}{4}$
$4.7\frac{1}{2}$
$\frac{5}{8}$

13.

$0.37\frac{3}{4}$
$5.43\frac{5}{6}$
$0.93\frac{1}{5}$
$9\frac{1}{8}$

14.

$\frac{5}{8}$
$0.6\frac{1}{4}$
$0.34\frac{3}{8}$
$45\frac{1}{4}$

15.

$0.45\frac{1}{2}$
$\frac{1}{16}$
$3.3\frac{1}{4}$
$4\frac{3}{16}$

ANSWERS

10. ________
11. ________
12. ________
13. ________
14. ________
15. ________
16. ________
17. ________

16. Jack Feiffer had the following quantities of paint stored in his garage: $2\frac{1}{2}$ gallons of burnt orange, $3\frac{1}{2}$ gallons of sky blue, $4\frac{1}{4}$ gallons of royal blue, $1\frac{3}{4}$ gallons of bright yellow, and $5\frac{1}{4}$ gallons of beige. How much paint is stored in Jack's garage?

17. In the last six days, production defects produced the following quantities of filament wrap that were unusable: Monday—$37\frac{2}{3}$ yards; Tuesday—$15\frac{5}{11}$ yards; Wednesday—$5\frac{5}{6}$ yards; Thursday—$12\frac{7}{8}$ yards; Friday—$8\frac{1}{4}$ yards; Saturday—$13\frac{3}{5}$ yards. What was the total amount of defective wrap produced? (Rename all fractions in decimal form to the nearest thousandth of a yard.)

NAME DATE

SKILL BUILDER 11B

Subtracting Common Fractions and Mixed Numbers

As in addition, like denominators must be used in order to subtract fractions. Subtract the numerator of the subtrahend from the numerator of the minuend. The common denominator of the two fractions will be the denominator of the difference. Rename in lowest terms if necessary.

$$\begin{array}{rcr} \frac{7}{8} & = & \frac{7}{8} \\ -\frac{3}{4} & = & \frac{6}{8} \\ \hline & & \frac{1}{8} \end{array}$$

When mixed numbers are subtracted, the fraction in the subtrahend may be larger than the fraction in the minuend. If so, subtract one unit from the whole number in the minuend and add it to the fraction in the minuend. Once the borrowing is accomplished, subtract the whole numbers and the numerators of the fractions.

$$\begin{array}{r} 9\frac{3}{8} \\ -5\frac{5}{8} \\ \hline \end{array} \quad \text{becomes} \quad \begin{array}{r} 8\frac{11}{8} \\ -5\frac{5}{8} \\ \hline 3\frac{6}{8} \end{array} \quad \text{or} \quad 3\frac{3}{4}$$

Find the difference in each problem. Rename in lowest terms, if necessary.

1. $24\frac{3}{8}$ − $11\frac{5}{6}$
2. $35\frac{1}{12}$ − $13\frac{5}{12}$
3. $7\frac{2}{9}$ − $3\frac{5}{16}$
4. $54\frac{2}{5}$ − $39\frac{7}{10}$
5. $36\frac{6}{35}$ − $24\frac{4}{5}$
6. $5\frac{11}{22}$ − $2\frac{7}{12}$
7. $49\frac{1}{2}$ − $29\frac{19}{36}$
8. $24\frac{7}{27}$ − $10\frac{5}{6}$
9. $9\frac{1}{2}$ − $7\frac{17}{18}$
10. $8\frac{1}{2}$ − $6\frac{5}{8}$
11. $68\frac{5}{8}$ − $9\frac{15}{16}$
12. $44\frac{3}{16}$ − $14\frac{19}{48}$
13. $29\frac{2}{3}$ − $13\frac{1}{4}$
14. $68\frac{5}{8}$ − $36.37\frac{1}{2}$
15. $88\frac{1}{3}$ − $22\frac{1}{4}$

16. a. How much must be added to $\frac{1}{4}$ to get $\frac{1}{2}$?
    b. How much must be added to $\frac{3}{8}$ to get $\frac{7}{8}$?

ANSWERS

1. ________
2. ________
3. ________
4. ________
5. ________
6. ________
7. ________
8. ________
9. ________
10. ________
11. ________
12. ________
13. ________
14. ________
15. ________
16. a. ________
    b. ________

17. Subtract the amount in the Weight of Cart column from the gross weight to find the weight of the load in each cart. Then find the total weight of the five loads.

TRUMAN MINES, LTD.

	CART NO.	GROSS WEIGHT	WEIGHT OF CART	WEIGHT OF LOAD
a.	15	$3{,}856\frac{1}{2}$ lb	$1{,}609\frac{7}{8}$ lb	________
b.	22	4,516 lb	$1{,}637\frac{3}{4}$ lb	________
c.	26	$4{,}763\frac{1}{8}$ lb	$1{,}609\frac{7}{8}$ lb	________
d.	31	$4{,}873\frac{1}{4}$ lb	$1{,}609\frac{7}{8}$ lb	________
e.	35	$4{,}529\frac{7}{8}$ lb	$1{,}637\frac{3}{4}$ lb	________
			Total Wt.	________

18. Subtract the bucket weight from the gross weight of each catch to find the weight of the fish. Then find the total of the Weight of Fish column.

BABCOCK FISHERIES

	GROSS WEIGHT	BUCKET WEIGHT	WEIGHT OF FISH
a.	$327\frac{5}{16}$ lb	$42\frac{1}{2}$ lb	________
b.	$321\frac{5}{8}$ lb	$42\frac{1}{2}$ lb	________
c.	$337\frac{7}{8}$ lb	$45\frac{3}{4}$ lb	________
d.	$344\frac{1}{4}$ lb	$45\frac{3}{4}$ lb	________
e.	$323\frac{3}{8}$ lb	$42\frac{1}{2}$ lb	________
		Total Wt.	________

NAME DATE

SKILL BUILDER 12A

Multiplying Common Fractions

To multiply fractions, there is no need to convert denominators to like terms; any combination of factors can be multiplied. Multiply numerator by numerator and denominator by denominator. Rename the resulting product in its simplest terms. If an improper fraction results, change it to a mixed or whole number.

$$\frac{3}{4} \times \frac{4}{9} = \frac{12}{36} = \frac{1}{3}$$

If **cross factors** (the numerator of one fraction and the denominator of the other fraction) can be evenly divided before multiplying, do so in order to simplify the multiplication. This process of dividing cross factors is called **cancellation.** If either the multiplicand or the multiplier is a whole number, express the whole number as that number over 1.

$$\frac{3}{\cancel{5}_1} \times \frac{\cancel{5}^1}{8} = \frac{3}{8} \qquad \frac{\cancel{3}^1}{\cancel{8}_4} \times \frac{\cancel{2}^1}{\cancel{9}_3} = \frac{1}{12} \qquad 5 \times \frac{2}{15} = \frac{\cancel{5}^1}{1} \times \frac{2}{\cancel{15}_3} = \frac{2}{3}$$

Find the products in the following problems. Rename the answers in simplest terms.

1. $\frac{5}{16} \times \frac{4}{15} =$
2. $\frac{8}{9} \times \frac{5}{24} =$
3. $\frac{7}{12} \times \frac{8}{49} =$
4. $\frac{5}{6} \times \frac{3}{4} =$
5. $\frac{4}{7} \times \frac{3}{7} =$
6. $3 \times \frac{5}{12} =$
7. $\frac{8}{27} \times 9 =$
8. $6 \times \frac{5}{18} =$
9. $\frac{3}{5} \times \frac{2}{3} =$
10. $\frac{2}{5} \times \frac{3}{10} =$
11. $5 \times \frac{3}{25} =$
12. $\frac{5}{8} \times \frac{9}{16} =$
13. $\frac{1}{2} \times \frac{3}{8} =$
14. $7 \times \frac{4}{21} =$
15. $\frac{11}{25} \times \frac{10}{33} =$
16. $\frac{8}{21} \times \frac{3}{16} \times \frac{2}{5} =$
17. $\frac{5}{34} \times \frac{4}{15} \times \frac{7}{8} =$
18. $\frac{8}{51} \times \frac{3}{16} \times \frac{5}{12} =$

19. Beame, Alvin, and Elder formed a partnership to market Worldwide Distributors. They agreed to take a share of the profits each month for personal expenses and to put the balance back into the business. The shares agreed upon were $\frac{2}{5}$, $\frac{1}{4}$, and $\frac{1}{8}$, respectively. The gross profit for the month of June was $22,520.

a. What fraction of the gross profit did their combined shares equal?

b. What fraction of the gross profit did they put back into the business?

c. What was the value of each of their shares?

ANSWERS

1. ________
2. ________
3. ________
4. ________
5. ________
6. ________
7. ________
8. ________
9. ________
10. ________
11. ________
12. ________
13. ________
14. ________
15. ________
16. ________
17. ________
18. ________
19. a. ________
b. ________
c. ________
____
____

20. Rabin Market's monthly expenses are $24,000. Of this $24,000, $\frac{1}{3}$ is for salaries, $\frac{1}{16}$ is for utilities, $\frac{1}{8}$ is for advertising, and $\frac{1}{12}$ is for general maintenance. What is the expense each month for the following?

a. Salaries
b. Utilities
c. Advertising
d. General maintenance

21. Hilary Antell operates a chicken farm on part of her 624-acre property. The house, barn, and roads presently occupy $\frac{1}{5}$ of the total acreage; chicken coops and runs occupy $\frac{2}{9}$ of the total. She plans to devote $\frac{1}{4}$ of the total acreage to fruit trees and the balance to vegetable fields.

a. How many acres will the fruit trees occupy?
b. What fraction of the total will be devoted to vegetable fields?

22. Andrew Porter died without leaving a will. Under the laws of his state, $\frac{1}{2}$ of his personal estate goes to his widow and the remainder is divided equally among his eight children. The estate has a value of $284,800.

a. How much would Porter's widow receive?
b. How much would each child receive?

23. The City of Laird has an opportunity to purchase land for a park. The section in question measures $\frac{7}{8}$ mile by $\frac{5}{12}$ mile.

a. If there are 640 acres to the square mile, how many acres are contained in this plot?
b. When federal funds were withdrawn, the city had only enough money to buy $77\frac{1}{9}$ of the available land. How many acres were they unable to buy?

24. A rule of thumb says that your monthly mortgage payment, including interest, should not exceed $\frac{7}{25}$ of your gross monthly income.

a. Bruce Angler earns $43,500 a year. How much of a mortgage payment can he afford per month?
b. Yvette Saunders earns $51,800 a year. How much of a mortgage payment can she afford per month?

25. Widget Industries have rented booth space at the International Trade Show Center. In the past they have spent $\frac{7}{16}$ of every dollar on exhibit construction and space rental, $\frac{1}{8}$ for transportation, $\frac{11}{32}$ on specialty advertising and personnel, and the balance on cleanup and removal of the exhibit after the show. If they have budgeted $228,000 for the coming show, how much will they spend on each of these items?

ANSWERS

20. a. ____________
b. ____________
c. ____________
d. ____________

21. a. ____________
b. ____________

22. a. ____________
b. ____________

23. a. ____________
b. ____________

24. a. ____________
b. ____________

25. a. ____________
b. ____________
c. ____________
d. ____________

NAME DATE

SKILL BUILDER 12B

Multiplying Mixed Numbers

To multiply mixed numbers, rename the factors as improper fractions. Use cancellation if possible, and rename the answer in lowest terms.

$$3\tfrac{3}{8} \times 2\tfrac{4}{9} = \frac{27}{8} \times \frac{22}{9}$$

$$\frac{\overset{3}{\cancel{27}}}{\underset{4}{\cancel{8}}} \times \frac{\overset{11}{\cancel{22}}}{\underset{1}{\cancel{9}}} = \frac{3}{4} \times \frac{11}{1} = \frac{33}{4} = 8\tfrac{1}{4}$$

Decimal fractions may be multiplied by common fractions and mixed numbers.

$$\$24.16 \times 2\tfrac{1}{4} = \frac{\overset{6.04}{\cancel{\$24.16}}}{1} \times \frac{9}{\underset{1}{\cancel{4}}} = \frac{\$54.36}{1} = \$54.36$$

Find the product in each of the following problems. Show the details of your work, and check each product.

1. $12\tfrac{1}{4} \times 2\tfrac{2}{7} =$
2. $24\tfrac{1}{4} \times 15\tfrac{1}{3} =$
3. $36\tfrac{2}{3} \times 21\tfrac{3}{8} =$
4. $12\tfrac{7}{8} \times 6\tfrac{3}{4} =$
5. $3\tfrac{1}{3} \times 4\tfrac{1}{8} =$
6. $6\tfrac{3}{4} \times 1\tfrac{1}{9} =$
7. $8\tfrac{1}{6} \times 2\tfrac{1}{7} =$
8. $11\tfrac{1}{4} \times 1\tfrac{1}{15} =$
9. $1\tfrac{1}{2} \times 2\tfrac{5}{6} =$
10. $6\tfrac{1}{2} \times 3\tfrac{1}{4} =$
11. $2\tfrac{1}{3} \times 3\tfrac{1}{2} =$
12. $3\tfrac{1}{3} \times 4\tfrac{1}{5} =$
13. Last year Joe Larson jogged $3\tfrac{5}{8}$ miles each day. Now he jogs $2\tfrac{1}{2}$ times this distance. How many miles does he now run each day?

ANSWERS

1. ____________
2. ____________
3. ____________
4. ____________
5. ____________
6. ____________
7. ____________
8. ____________
9. ____________
10. ____________
11. ____________
12. ____________
13. ____________

14. The current market value of May Johnson's stocks are listed below. What is the value of her investment in each stock, and what is the total value of her portfolio? (In computing your answers, change any fractional parts of a dollar to cents, rounding off to 3 decimal places, where necessary.)

a. Stock A—54 shares @ $\$48\frac{1}{8}$ a share
b. Stock B—300 shares @ $\$12\frac{5}{8}$ a share.
c. Stock C—80 shares @ $\$39\frac{1}{2}$ a share.
d. Stock D—84 shares @ $\$68\frac{7}{8}$ a share.
e. Stock E—312 shares @ $\$32\frac{3}{4}$ a share.
f. Total

ANSWERS

14. a. __________
b. __________
c. __________
d. __________
e. __________
f. __________
15. __________
16. __________
17. __________
18. __________

15. Harry Wilson uses his car for business. Last year he drove 21,876 miles, using $1{,}393\frac{4}{10}$ gallons of gasoline. If the average price per gallon was $\$1.05\frac{9}{10}$ a gallon, how much did he spend on gasoline (round off your final answer to the nearest cent)?

16. The Hardings are ordering new carpeting costing \$24.75 a square yard (\$2.75 a square foot). The areas to be carpeted are the living room, $21\frac{1}{2}$ ft long by $18\frac{1}{4}$ ft wide; and the dining room, $18\frac{1}{4}$ ft long by $14\frac{3}{4}$ ft wide. What will be the total cost of carpet for these rooms? (Multiply length times width to get area. Determine the total area first; then work out the cost. Round off your answer to the nearest cent.)

17. For each pound of pistachio nuts purchased, Taft's Nuts is offering customers an extra $\frac{1}{4}$ pound free. Alice Garfield bought 5 pounds of the nuts. How many pounds will she get free?

18. Lucy Ford has been hired by the Carter Corporation to do odd jobs. She will be paid \$8.50 an hour. On Monday, she worked $4\frac{1}{2}$ hours. On Tuesday, she worked $6\frac{1}{4}$ hours. On Friday, she worked $3\frac{3}{4}$ hours. How much did she earn for the three days that she worked?

NAME DATE

SKILL BUILDER 13A

Dividing Common Fractions

To divide common fractions, invert (turn upside down) the divisor and multiply. Rename the quotient in simplest terms. When either the dividend or the divisor is a whole number, write it as that number over 1 before dividing. Do not use cancellation until *after* the divisor has been inverted.

$$\frac{3}{5} \div \frac{9}{16} = \frac{\overset{1}{\cancel{3}}}{5} \times \frac{16}{\underset{3}{\cancel{9}}} = \frac{16}{15} = 1\frac{1}{15}$$

$$4 \div \frac{2}{9} = \frac{4}{1} \div \frac{2}{9} = \frac{\overset{2}{\cancel{4}}}{1} \times \frac{9}{\underset{1}{\cancel{2}}} = \frac{18}{1} = 18$$

$$\frac{5}{12} \div 3 = \frac{5}{12} \div \frac{3}{1} = \frac{5}{12} \times \frac{1}{3} = \frac{5}{36}$$

Find the quotients in the following problems. Rename the answers in simplest terms if necessary.

1. $\frac{3}{8} \div \frac{7}{9}$
2. $\frac{2}{7} \div \frac{4}{11}$
3. $\frac{5}{12} \div 15$
4. $\frac{5}{6} \div \frac{5}{12}$
5. $\frac{3}{16} \div \frac{5}{8}$
6. $25 \div \frac{5}{9}$
7. $\frac{16}{35} \div \frac{2}{7}$
8. $\frac{5}{24} \div \frac{3}{10}$
9. $12 \div \frac{3}{8}$
10. $\frac{14}{17} \div 21$
11. $\frac{3}{4} \div \frac{9}{32}$
12. $\frac{12}{57} \div \frac{2}{3}$
13. $\frac{5}{9} \div \frac{5}{18}$
14. $\frac{2}{5} \div \frac{28}{31}$
15. $\frac{5}{36} \div \frac{4}{9}$
16. $\frac{9}{16} \div \frac{7}{18}$
17. $42 \div \frac{18}{25}$
18. $\frac{7}{8} \div \frac{5}{32}$

ANSWERS

1. ____________
2. ____________
3. ____________
4. ____________
5. ____________
6. ____________
7. ____________
8. ____________
9. ____________
10. ____________
11. ____________
12. ____________
13. ____________
14. ____________
15. ____________
16. ____________
17. ____________
18. ____________

ANSWERS

19.	a.	________
	b.	________
20.		________
21.		________
22.		________
23.		________
24.		________

19. Lloyd King is a top sales representative for Global Safety Products. Last month his sales expenses amounted to $4,800, which represented $\frac{3}{32}$ of his sales for the month.

a. What was the value of Lloyd's sales for the month?

b. Lloyd's commission is $\frac{2}{15}$ of his net sales (total sales less expenses) for the month. What was the amount of his commission to the nearest cent for that same month?

20. Environetics' design engineer has developed an energy-saving light requiring a platinum ribbon. The platinum ribbon comes from a roll 174 inches long. Each ribbon must be $\frac{3}{32}$ inch long. How many ribbons can be cut from the roll?

21. Rita Garland wishes to tile her 18 foot by 15 foot recreation room with a 9-inch by 9-inch tile. How many whole tiles will she need to do the job?

22. Matt Carlson has a garden plot measuring 162 feet by 162 feet. He is planning to plant rows of seeds $\frac{3}{4}$ of a yard apart, planting as many rows as possible. How many rows will he be able to plant?

23. Deborah Donner is cutting ribbon from 15-foot rolls. Each ribbon will be $\frac{3}{4}$ foot long. If she needs 220 ribbons in all, how many 15-foot rolls will she need?

24. A farmer sold 48 baskets of tomatoes for $4.50 a basket. The farmer used the proceeds, which amounted to $\frac{2}{3}$ of the total cost, toward the purchase of seedlings. How much did the farmer spend on seedlings?

NAME DATE

SKILL BUILDER 13B

Dividing Mixed Numbers

Mixed numbers can be divided by first changing them to improper fractions. Then invert the divisor and multiply. Before multiplying, be sure to perform any cancellation possible. Rename the resulting quotient in its simplest terms.

$$15\tfrac{3}{8} \div 5\tfrac{1}{4} = \frac{123}{8} \div \frac{21}{4} = \frac{\overset{41}{\cancel{123}}}{\underset{2}{\cancel{8}}} \times \frac{\overset{1}{\cancel{4}}}{\underset{7}{\cancel{21}}} = \frac{41}{14} = 2\tfrac{13}{14}$$

$$7\tfrac{2}{3} \div 4 = \frac{23}{3} \div \frac{4}{1} = \frac{23}{3} \times \frac{1}{4} = \frac{23}{12} = 1\tfrac{11}{12}$$

Decimal fractions may be divided by common fractions and mixed numbers.

$$\$15.85 \div 3\tfrac{4}{9} = \frac{\$15.85}{1} \div \frac{31}{9} = \frac{\$15.85}{1} \times \frac{9}{31} = \frac{\$142.65}{31} = \$4.601 \rightarrow \$4.60$$

$$6\tfrac{2}{3} \div 7.63 = \frac{20}{3} \div \frac{7.63}{1} = \frac{20}{3} \times \frac{1}{7.63} = \frac{20}{22.89} = 0.87374$$

Find the quotients in the following problems. Show the details of your work. In problems 13 to 18, you may want to change the decimal fractions to common fractions. If not, round off your final answers to 4 decimal places, where necessary.

1. $32\tfrac{1}{6} \div 10\tfrac{2}{3}$
2. $24\tfrac{3}{5} \div 8\tfrac{1}{5}$
3. $5\tfrac{1}{8} \div 2\tfrac{2}{9}$
4. $1\tfrac{2}{3} \div 1\tfrac{2}{3}$
5. $16\tfrac{3}{4} \div 15\tfrac{2}{5}$
6. $12\tfrac{1}{2} \div 8\tfrac{1}{3}$
7. $12\tfrac{3}{5} \div \dfrac{3}{4}$
8. $36\tfrac{2}{3} \div 9$
9. $24\tfrac{1}{2} \div 8\tfrac{3}{4}$
10. $51\tfrac{5}{12} \div 12\tfrac{2}{5}$
11. $26 \div 3\tfrac{3}{8}$
12. $48\tfrac{1}{2} \div \dfrac{7}{8}$

ANSWERS

1. ________
2. ________
3. ________
4. ________
5. ________
6. ________
7. ________
8. ________
9. ________
10. ________
11. ________
12. ________

13. $0.625 \div 1\frac{4}{9}$

14. $0.375 \div 5\frac{1}{2}$

15. $0.25 \div 22\frac{3}{8}$

16. $0.75 \div 41\frac{1}{3}$

17. $0.125 \div \frac{1}{3}$

18. $0.4 \div 12\frac{1}{4}$

19. Canteen Cooperative serves soup as part of its daily menu. The soup is packed in cans containing 46 ounces each; the average portion size is $7\frac{1}{3}$ ounces. On an average day, 125 portions of soup are served. To the nearest whole can, how many cans of soup are used each day?

20. Betty Giddens works in the cutting rooms of an exclusive women's clothing manufacturer. Her next work order is a piece of fabric $128\frac{3}{8}$ yards long, from which she must cut skirts requiring $2\frac{1}{4}$ yards each. How many skirts will she be able to cut from this piece of fabric? Hint: Round down your answer to the nearest whole unit.

21. Richard Mullin paid \$9,481.75 for the purchase of common stock. The purchase price was $\$48\frac{7}{8}$ a share. How many shares of stock did he purchase?

22. One package of natural cereal costs 63 cents for $7\frac{1}{2}$ ounces. Another costs \$1.39 for $18\frac{3}{4}$ ounces.

a. What is the price of one ounce to the nearest tenth of a cent in the smaller package?

b. What is the price of one ounce to the nearest tenth of a cent in the larger package?

23. The city of Alexandria is planning a $22\frac{1}{4}$ mile long bus route. If a bus stop is placed every mile and a half, how many stops will be on the route? (Round off your answer to the nearest whole number.)

ANSWERS

13. ____________

14. ____________

15. ____________

16. ____________

17. ____________

18. ____________

19. ____________

20. ____________

21. ____________

22. ____________

____

23. ____________

NAME DATE

SKILL BUILDER — Computing Aliquot Parts — 14A

Any number that can be divided evenly into another number is known as an **aliquot part** of that number.

Example: What part of \$1, or 100 cents, is $37\frac{1}{2}$ cents?

Solution: Place $37\frac{1}{2}$ cents over 100 cents and rename the fraction in its simplest terms.

$$37\tfrac{1}{2} \div 100 = \frac{37\frac{1}{2}}{100} \quad \frac{2 \times 37\frac{1}{2}}{2 \times 100} = \frac{75}{200} = \frac{3}{8}$$

—or—

$$37\tfrac{1}{2} \div 100 = \frac{75}{2} \div \frac{100}{1} = \frac{\overset{3}{\cancel{75}}}{2} \times \frac{1}{\underset{4}{\cancel{100}}} = \frac{3}{8}$$

Example: What part of 44 is $5\frac{1}{2}$?

Solution: $5\frac{1}{2} \div 44 = \dfrac{5\frac{1}{2}}{44} = \dfrac{2 \times 5\frac{1}{2}}{2 \times 44} = \dfrac{11}{88} = \dfrac{1}{8}$

—or—

$$5\tfrac{1}{2} \div 44 = \frac{11}{2} \div \frac{44}{1} = \frac{\overset{1}{\cancel{11}}}{2} \times \frac{1}{\underset{4}{\cancel{44}}} = \frac{1}{8}$$

Many computations can be simplified by recognizing the aliquot parts of one or more of the terms and by using those values in place of the original figures in the computation.

For example, how much would it cost to purchase 1,264 metric converter slides at 25 cents each? Rather than multiply 1,264 by 25 cents, it should be recognized that 25 cents equals $\frac{1}{4}$ of \$1. If the items sold for \$1 each, the cost would be \$1,264. However, since they sold for 25 cents, or $\frac{1}{4}$ of a dollar, divide \$1,264 by 4 to obtain a purchase cost of \$316.

Example: Find the cost of 432 items at $37\frac{1}{2}$ cents each.

Solution: $37\frac{1}{2}$¢ $= \frac{3}{8}$ of \$1 $\quad \dfrac{\overset{54}{\cancel{432}}}{1} \times \dfrac{3}{\underset{1}{\cancel{8}}} = \$162$

Find the aliquot parts of \$1 represented by the following amounts. Show details of your work.

1. 50¢ = __________ of \$1
2. $6\frac{1}{4}$¢ = __________ of \$1
3. $8\frac{1}{3}$¢ = __________ of \$1
4. $33\frac{1}{3}$¢ = __________ of \$1
5. $87\frac{1}{2}$¢ = __________ of \$1
6. $37\frac{1}{2}$¢ = __________ of \$1
7. 25¢ = __________ of \$1
8. $12\frac{1}{2}$¢ = __________ of \$1
9. 75¢ = __________ of \$1
10. $16\frac{2}{3}$¢ = __________ of \$1
11. $83\frac{1}{3}$¢ = __________ of \$1
12. $62\frac{1}{2}$¢ = __________ of \$1

Using the methods shown on page 58, find the cost of each of the following purchases.

13. 408 qt @ $16\frac{2}{3}$¢ = ______ **14.** 368 in @ $6\frac{1}{4}$¢ = ______ **15.** 735 in @ $33\frac{1}{3}$¢ = ______

16. 252 in @ $12\frac{1}{2}$¢ = ______ **17.** 1,272 qt @ $66\frac{2}{3}$¢ = ______ **18.** 492 qt @ $8\frac{1}{3}$¢ = ______

Aliquot parts can be used to find the quantity of items bought when the unit price and the total cost are known.

Example: Jean McCrea, a candidate for public office, spent \$108 for monogrammed pencils to be given to prospective voters. The pencils cost $12\frac{1}{2}$ cents each. How many pencils were bought?

Solution:

$12\frac{1}{2}¢ = \frac{1}{8}$ of \$1 $\quad \$108 \div \frac{1}{8} = \frac{108}{1} \times \frac{8}{1} = 864$ pencils

Example: Cotton cloth costs $87\frac{1}{2}$¢ a yard. If a total purchase came to \$203, how many yards were bought?

Solution:

$87\frac{1}{2}¢ = \frac{7}{8}$ of \$1

$\$203 \div \frac{7}{8} = \frac{\cancel{203}^{29}}{1} \times \frac{8}{\cancel{7}_{1}} = 232$ yards

What quantities would be purchased in each of the following problems?

19. \$70 for decals at $8\frac{1}{3}$¢ each = __________ decals

20. \$213.50 for paint thinner at $87\frac{1}{2}$¢ a pint = __________ pints

21. \$135 for felt at $93\frac{3}{4}$¢ a meter = __________ meters

22. \$168 for rice flour at 50¢ a pound = __________ pounds

23. \$225 for orange juice at 75¢ a quart = __________ quarts

24. John Rolfe paid \$1.25 a quart for automatic transmission fluid. His total bill came to \$15.00. How many quarts did he purchase? 24. __________

25. Ty Keller paid 87.5 cents a pint for brake fluid. His total bill came to \$71.75. How many pints did he purchase?

25. __________

NAME DATE

SKILL BUILDER — Using Aliquot Parts — 14B

Aliquot parts are useful only if their values and relationships are recognized quickly. The list below shows the aliquot parts of \$1 which are used most frequently. Use it as necessary for the problems below.

$\$\frac{1}{2} = 50¢$ $\$\frac{1}{5} = 20¢$ $\$\frac{1}{8} = 12\frac{1}{2}¢$ $\$\frac{7}{10} = 70¢$

$\$\frac{1}{3} = 33\frac{1}{3}¢$ $\$\frac{2}{5} = 40¢$ $\$\frac{3}{8} = 37\frac{1}{2}¢$ $\$\frac{9}{10} = 90¢$

$\$\frac{2}{3} = 66\frac{2}{3}¢$ $\$\frac{3}{5} = 60¢$ $\$\frac{5}{8} = 62\frac{1}{2}¢$ $\$\frac{1}{12} = 8\frac{1}{3}¢$

$\$\frac{1}{4} = 25¢$ $\$\frac{4}{5} = 80¢$ $\$\frac{7}{8} = 87\frac{1}{2}¢$ $\$\frac{1}{16} = 6\frac{1}{4}¢$

$\$\frac{3}{4} = 75¢$ $\$\frac{1}{6} = 16\frac{2}{3}¢$ $\$\frac{1}{10} = 10¢$ $\$\frac{1}{20} = 5¢$

$\$\frac{5}{6} = 83\frac{1}{3}¢$ $\$\frac{3}{10} = 30¢$

Find the total cost of each of the following groups of purchases. In the parentheses after each price, show what aliquot part of \$1 that price represents. Round off your answers to the nearest cent where necessary.

1. 128 qt @ $12\frac{1}{2}¢$ ( ) = ______
   360 qt @ $16\frac{2}{3}¢$ ( ) = ______
   252 qt @ $83\frac{1}{3}¢$ ( ) = ______
   486 qt @ 40¢ ( ) = ______
   Total ______

2. 355 ft @ 60¢ ( ) = ______
   288 ft @ $12\frac{1}{2}¢$ ( ) = ______
   369 ft @ $33\frac{1}{3}¢$ ( ) = ______
   127 ft @ 75¢ ( ) = ______
   Total ______

3. 300 yd @ $62\frac{1}{2}¢$ ( ) = ______
   364 yd @ 25¢ ( ) = ______
   112 yd @ $37\frac{1}{2}¢$ ( ) = ______
   415 yd @ $33\frac{1}{3}¢$ ( ) = ______
   Total ______

4. 286 lb @ $66\frac{2}{3}¢$ ( ) = ______
   280 lb @ 20¢ ( ) = ______
   720 lb @ $66\frac{2}{3}¢$ ( ) = ______
   752 lb @ $6\frac{1}{4}¢$ ( ) = ______
   Total ______

Aliquot parts can be used to speed up computations for values greater than one dollar, too.

320 pieces at \$1.12½ each

$12\frac{1}{2}¢ = \frac{1}{8}$ of \$1

$320 \times \$1 = \$320$

$+320 \times \frac{1}{8} = +40$

\$360

256 units at \$37.50 each

$\$37.50 = \frac{3}{8}$ of \$100

$\frac{256}{1} \times \frac{3}{8} = 96$

$96 \times 100 = \$9{,}600$

112 items at \$6.25 each

$\$6.25 = \frac{5}{8}$ of \$10

$\frac{112}{1} \times \frac{5}{8} = 70$

$70 \times \$10 = \$700$

Compute the extensions on the following purchases using aliquot parts for all values. In the parentheses after the unit price, show the fraction of \$10, \$100, and so on, that the price represents. Round off to the nearest cent where necessary. Then find the totals.

5. 42 Jackets at $62.50 each (   ) = ________

74 Wool shirts at $12.50 each (   ) = ________

116 Pairs socks at $6.25 each (   ) = ________

15 Pairs slacks at $25.00 each (   ) = ________

48 Knit shirts at $8.33 each (   ) = ________

13 Sport suits at $90.00 each (   ) = ________

Total ________

6. 18 Radios at $37.50 each (   ) = ________

15 Record albums at $8.33 each (   ) = ________

12 tapes at $6.25 each (   ) = ________

23 Compact Discs at $8.75 each (   ) = ________

60 Carrying cases at $8.33 each (   ) = ________

87 Video tapes at $3.75 each (   ) = ________

Total ________

7. 46 Brushes at $6.25 each (   ) = ________

48 Paint boxes at $9.00 each (   ) = ________

32 Cans paint thinner at $6.25 each (   ) = ________

24 Clay pots at $16.67 each (   ) = ________

18 Portable easels at $8.75 each (   ) = ________

20 Palettes at $12.50 each (   ) = ________

10 Sheets sand paper at $0.50 each (   ) = ________

Total = ________

8. 26 Wrench sets at $37.50 each (   ) = ________

52 Drills at $12.50 each (   ) = ________

318 Screw packs at $6.25 each (   ) = ________

6 Socket sets at $37.50 each (   ) = ________

12 Entrance locks at $16.67 each (   ) = ________

15 Latch sets at $8.33 each (   ) = ________

10 Ratchet sets at $6.25 each (   ) = ________

Total ________

NAME DATE

SKILL BUILDER — Electronic Calculators — 15A

The electronic calculator can be a very helpful tool, but does not replace an understanding of how problems are to be solved. Many very good calculators can be purchased for under ten dollars, and are either battery or solar powered. The cost of battery replacement is one factor which should be considered in the purchase decision. Most of these inexpensive calculators contain the same features, and operate in a similar fashion.

The key pad will usually contain the following functions keys:

[On/Off]	usually found only on battery operated units.
[+], [−], [×], [÷]	The basic functions of **addition, subtraction, multiplication,** and **division.**
[·]	**Decimal point**
[=]	**Equals**
[C]	**Clear**—this key clears all the content of the calculator except the memory.
[CE]	**Clear entry**—clears only the numbers showing on the display.
[%]	**Percent key** automatically positions the decimal point in percent computations.

Memory Section—3 or 4 Keys

[M+]	**Adds** numbers to the memory section.
[M−]	**Subtracts** numbers from the memory section.
[MR]	**Memory recall**—brings the total from the memory section to be used in computation.
[MC]	**Memory clear**—clears the entire content of the memory section.
[R-CM]	**Recall/Clear memory**—combines the MR and MC keys in a 3 key memory section. Pressed once, the memory content is **recalled;** pressed twice, and the memory content is **cleared,** or **erased.**

You may also have these key functions on your calculator:

[+/−]	**Sign change**—this key will convert a negative (minus) value to a positive (plus) value, and also from positive to negative.
[√]	**Square Root key**
[$\frac{1}{X}$]	**Reciprocal key**
[X^2]	**Square key**

These last three keys will seldom be used in usual business computations.

Generally, computations are made in the same order as written. It is also good procedure to clear both memory and operating sections before starting any computations. The **equals key (=)** need only be used at the end of the computation.

Example: Add 153, 287, 61, 103, and 1,005.

Solution:
[C] 153 [+] 287 [+] 61 [+] 103 [+] 1,005 [=] 1,609

Example: Subtract 128, 51, and 1,007 from 4,873.

Solution: [C] 4,873 [−] 128 [−] 51 [−] 1,007 [=] 3,687

In **multiplication,** either the multiplier or multiplicand can be entered first. The order of entry does not change the end result.

Example: Multiply 528 by 107

Solution: [C] 528 [×] 107 [=] 56,496

If the same multiplier is to be used several times, entering this number first (the constant) will eliminate the need to reenter the constant multiplier. After the first multiplication is complete, enter the next multiplicand and press the equals key, and so on.

Example: Multiply 459 × 132; 6,870 × 132; and 10,103 × 132

Solution: [C] 132 [×] 459 [=] 60,588
6,870 [=] 906,840
10,103 [=] 1,333,596

In **division,** always enter the **dividend** first, and then the **divisor.**

Example: Divide 5,616 by 26

Solution: [C] 5,616 [÷] 26 [=] 216

When working with decimal fractions, all numbers are entered with the decimal point properly placed. The calculator automatically adjusts the decimal point placement in the solution.

Example: Add 101.37, 5,018, 1.006, and 97

Solution:
[C] 101.37 [+] 5,018 [+] 1.006 [+] 97 [=] 5,217.376

Example: Subtract 146.0972 from 512.02

Solution: [C] 512.02 [−] 146.0972 [=] 365.9228

Example: Multiply 41.79 by 2.0013

Solution: [C] 41.79 [×] 2.0013 [=] 83.634327

Example: Divide 32.8 by 0.044

Solution: [C] 32.8 [÷] .044 [=] 745.45454

The **memory** section of the calculator makes it possible to store numbers to be used in later computations, or to total the results of a series of computations. Numbers are added to the memory by pressing **M+**, and are subtracted from the memory by pressing **M−**. To utilize the memory function, perform the indicated computations, and when the answer is obtained, press **M+**. Each time this is done, the latest number answer will be added to the memory total. Likewise, if the answer is to be subtracted from the memory total, press **M−**, and this will reduce the memory total by that amount. The **M+** or **M−** key can be used in place of the equals key (=).

Example: Add the following groups of numbers, finding a total for each group, and then the grand total.

a.	b.	c.
315	85	59
426	106	18
515	39	112

Solution:
a. [C] 315 [+] 426 [+] 515 [M+] 1,256
b. [C] 85 [+] 106 [+] 39 [M+] 230
c. [C] 59 [+] 18 [+] 112 [M+] 189
Grand Total [MR] or [R-CM] 1,675

The same procedure would be followed to accumulate quotients and products.

When using the **percent key,** it is not necessary to convert a percent to its decimal form. The percent key can also be used to replace the equals key (=).

Example: What is 25% of 300?

Solution: [C] 300 [×] 25 [%] 75

Example: $87.50 is 62.5% of what amount?

Solution: [C] 87.5 [÷] 62.5 [%] 140

Example: 66 is what percent of 300?

Solution: [C] 66 [÷] 300 [%] 22

Mixed calculations occur when several different calculations are to be carried out in the same problem. This will require using the memory function and performing the right combinations of computations.

Example: Add 3 × 12, 7 × 26, 5 × 31, minus 119

Solution: [C] 3 [×] 12 [M+] 7 [×] 26 [M+] 5 [×] 31 [M+] 119 [M−] [R-CM] 254

Example: $\frac{(45 + 23) \times (48 \div 17) + 6}{35}$

Solution: [C] 45 [+] 23 [M+] 48 [÷] 17 [×] [R-CM] [+] 6 [÷] 35 [=] 5.657

It is sometimes helpful to perform the operations shown in the denominator first, and then place this result in memory as the divisor.

Example: $\frac{\$203}{\$8,700 \times 96/360} = ?$

Solution: [C] 8,700 [×] 96 [÷] 360 [M+] 203 [÷] [R-CM] [%] 8.75

NAME DATE

SKILL BUILDER 15B

Electronic Calculator Application Problems

Using the methods described in Skill Builder 15a, do the following problems.

1. Add each of the following and show a grand total.

a.	b.	c.	d.
484	327	35	738
189	106	583	804
687	947	120	514
319	625	890	663

2. Find the product for each of the following, and the total of all products.

a. 425×87 b. 1.096×327 c. $1{,}859 \times 0.92$ d. 12.82×3.04

3. Find the quotient for each of the following, and the total of all quotients. Carry your answer to the capacity of your calculator (usually 8 places in total).

a. $99.52 \div 74 =$ b. $251.8 \div 141.26 =$

c. $14.186 \div 0.088 =$ d. $3.93 \div 5.268 =$

4. $\dfrac{(14 + 86) \times (152 \div 4) - 77}{6.25} =$

5. $\dfrac{(48 \div 6) + (852 \div 8) - (72 \div 3)}{5} =$

6. What is $87\frac{1}{2}\%$ of \$500?

ANSWERS

1. a. ________
b. ________
c. ________
d. ________
Grand Total ________
2. a. ________
b. ________
c. ________
d. ________
Grand Total ________
3. a. ________
b. ________
c. ________
d. ________
Grand Total ________
4. ________
5. ________
6. ________

7. 123 is $37\frac{1}{2}\%$ of what number?

8. What percent of 9,200 is 460?

9. $(12 \times 5) + 12$ is what percent of 360?

10. $(147 \div 49) \times (248 \times \frac{1}{2}\%) - .72 =$

11. $\dfrac{(2 \times 12) \times 2{,}240}{7{,}000 \times (48 + 1)} =$

12. $\dfrac{\$5{,}000 \times 18\% \times \frac{1}{12}}{2} =$

13. $\$991 + (48 \times \$192.50) - \$7{,}991 =$

14. A riding lawnmower is list priced at $485 less trade discounts of 30%, 10%, and 5%. What is the cost of the mower?

15. Shirts cost $6 each, and are marked up 52% on cost. What is the selling price for each shirt?

16. What are the total earnings for an employee who worked 40 hours at $6.90 an hour, and $3\frac{1}{2}$ hours at time and one-half?

17. What would the rate of interest be if $885 of interest was paid on a loan of $15,000 for seven months?

18. The most that Steve can charge for a wool sweater is $55. His normal markup is 40% on selling price. What is the most he can pay for one of these sweaters?

19. FICA tax (Social Security) is paid at a rate of 7.51% by both the employer and employee. How much FICA tax would the employer pay for five employees whose gross earnings were $873, $912.50, $1,012, $895, and $1,175?

20. A three month note for $7,500 earning interest at 11% is discounted at a rate of 15% after one month. What are the proceeds on this note (Face Value + Interest − Discount = Proceeds)?

ANSWERS

7. ________
8. ________
9. ________
10. ________
11. ________
12. ________
13. ________
14. ________
15. ________
16. ________
17. ________
18. ________
19. ________
20. ________

NAME DATE

SKILL BUILDER 16A

Reading Tables

READING TABLES A **table** is a systematic arrangement of information, usually numeric. The data is arranged in labeled rows and columns. Tables are read by selecting the row and column containing the information sought. The data required is found at the intersection of the row and the column. Tables are often used in business to provide a clear and concise presentation of data.

SOCIAL SECURITY TAX TABLES Social Security Tax (FICA) is withheld from most workers' earnings to pay for retirement and disability pensions. Tables like the one shown are used to calculate the amount withheld from each employee's check.

Example: How much FICA tax would be withheld from earnings of $81.47?

Solution: Read down the wages column until the correct bracket is reached. $81.47 is at least $81.43 but less than $81.56. Read across this row to the Tax to be withheld column. The tax is $6.12.

The main table provides tax brackets only up to $99.99. A box in the bottom right corner gives the tax withheld on multiples of $100. The tax on the amount less than $100 is added to the tax on $100 or a multiple of $100 to find the total amount withheld.

Example: Steve Kiernan earned $283 during his last pay period. How much FICA tax is to be withheld?

Solution: First find the tax on $83. This amount is contained in the tax bracket of at least $82.89 but less than $83.03. The tax for this bracket is $6.23. Use the bottom corner of the table to find the tax on $200. The tax to be withheld is $15.02. Add the two tax amounts to find the total tax to be withheld.

$ 6.23	Tax on $83
15.02	Tax on $200
$21.25	Total tax withheld

Social Security Employee Tax Table
7.51% employee tax deductions

Wages at least	But less than	Tax to be withheld	Wages at least	But less than	Tax to be withheld
76.37	76.50	5.74	89.02	89.15	6.69
76.50	76.64	5.75	89.15	89.29	6.70
76.64	76.77	5.76	89.29	89.42	6.71
76.77	76.90	5.77	89.42	89.55	6.72
76.90	77.04	5.78	89.55	89.69	6.73
77.04	77.17	5.79	89.69	89.82	6.74
77.17	77.30	5.80	89.82	89.95	6.75
77.30	77.44	5.81	89.95	90.08	6.76
77.44	77.57	5.82	90.08	90.22	6.77
77.57	77.70	5.83	90.22	90.35	6.78
77.70	77.83	5.84	90.35	90.48	6.79
77.83	77.97	5.85	90.48	90.62	6.80
77.97	78.10	5.86	90.62	90.75	6.81
78.10	78.23	5.87	90.75	90.88	6.82
78.23	78.37	5.88	90.88	91.02	6.83
78.37	78.50	5.89	91.02	91.15	6.84
78.50	78.63	5.90	91.15	91.28	6.85
78.63	78.77	5.91	91.28	91.42	6.86
78.77	78.90	5.92	91.42	91.55	6.87
78.90	79.03	5.93	91.55	91.68	6.88
79.03	79.17	5.94	91.68	91.82	6.89
79.17	79.30	5.95	91.82	91.95	6.90
79.30	79.43	5.96	91.95	92.08	6.91
79.43	79.57	5.97	92.08	92.22	6.92
79.57	79.70	5.98	92.22	92.35	6.93
79.70	79.83	5.99	92.35	92.48	6.94
79.83	79.97	6.00	92.48	92.61	6.95
79.97	80.10	6.01	92.61	92.75	6.96
80.10	80.23	6.02	92.75	92.88	6.97
80.23	80.36	6.03	92.88	93.01	6.98
80.36	80.50	6.04	93.01	93.15	6.99
80.50	80.63	6.05	93.15	93.28	7.00
80.63	80.76	6.06	93.28	93.41	7.01
80.76	80.90	6.07	93.41	93.55	7.02
80.90	81.03	6.08	93.55	93.68	7.03
81.03	81.16	6.09	93.68	93.81	7.04
81.16	81.30	6.10	93.81	93.95	7.05
81.30	81.43	6.11	93.95	94.08	7.06
81.43	81.56	6.12	94.08	94.21	7.07
81.56	81.70	6.13	94.21	94.35	7.08
81.70	81.83	6.14	94.35	94.48	7.09
81.83	81.96	6.15	94.48	94.61	7.10
81.96	82.10	6.16	94.61	94.75	7.11
82.10	82.23	6.17	94.75	94.88	7.12
82.23	82.36	6.18	94.88	95.01	7.13
82.36	82.50	6.19	95.01	95.14	7.14
82.50	82.63	6.20	95.14	95.28	7.15
82.63	82.76	6.21	95.28	95.41	7.16
82.76	82.89	6.22	95.41	95.54	7.17
82.89	83.03	6.23	95.54	95.68	7.18
83.03	83.16	6.24	95.68	95.81	7.19
83.16	83.29	6.25	95.81	95.94	7.20
83.29	83.43	6.26	95.94	96.08	7.21
83.43	83.56	6.27	96.08	96.21	7.22
83.56	83.69	6.28	96.21	96.34	7.23
83.69	83.83	6.29	96.34	96.48	7.24
83.83	83.96	6.30	96.48		
83.96	84.09	6.31	96.61	**Wages**	**Taxes**
84.09	84.23	6.32	96.74	100	$7.51
84.23	84.36	6.33	96.88	200	15.02
84.36	84.49	6.34	97.01	300	22.53
84.49	84.63	6.35	97.14	400	30.04
84.63	84.76	6.36	97.28	500	37.55
84.76	84.89	6.37	97.41	600	45.06
84.89	85.02	6.38	97.54	700	52.57
85.02	85.16	6.39	97.67	800	60.08
85.16	85.29	6.40	97.81	900	67.59
85.29	85.42	6.41	97.94	1,000	75.10
85.42	85.56	6.42	98.07		
85.56	85.69	6.43	98.21		

Determine the amount of FICA tax to be withheld from the following employees' gross earnings using the tax table on page 65.

	EMPLOYEE	GROSS EARNINGS
1.	Betz, Allan	$ 92.00
2.	Callahan, Betty	$295.00
3.	Fromkin, Helen	$484.52
4.	Jung, Kurt	$ 94.93
5.	Lawson, Lois	$179.85
6.	Meszaros, Timothy	$883.50

ANSWERS

1. ____________
2. ____________
3. ____________
4. ____________
5. ____________
6. ____________

FOURTH CLASS

PARCEL POST ZONED RATES
CONSULT POSTMASTER FOR WEIGHT AND SIZE LIMITS

NONMACHINABLE SURCHARGE:
A parcel mailed to a ZIP Code destination *outside* the BMC service area for your post office (shown below) is subject to a surcharge of $1 15 in addition to the rate shown below if

A It is nonmachinable according to the standards prescribed in Domestic Mail Manual section 753. *or*
B It weighs more than 35 pounds

INTRA-BMC RATE:
A parcel mailed from your local post office to a ZIP Code destination within its BMC service area (shown below) is eligible for a discount of $0 20 from the rate shown below

INTRA-BMC ZIP CODE DESTINATIONS FOR YOUR POST OFFICE:

Note If the Intra-BMC ZIP Code destinations for your post office are not shown above. consult your local Postmaster and write the ZIP Codes in the space provided

Weight, up to but not exceeding— (pounds)		*Zones*						
	Local	*1 & 2*	*3*	*4*	*5*	*6*	*7*	*8*
2	$1.63	$1.69	$1.81	$1.97	$2.24	$2.35	$2.35	$2.35
3	1.68	1.78	1.95	2.20	2.59	2.98	3.42	4.25
4	1.74	1.86	2.10	2.42	2.94	3.46	4.05	5.25
5	1.79	1.95	2.24	2.65	3.29	3.94	4.57	6.25
6	1.85	2.04	2.39	2.87	3.64	4.43	5.30	7.34
7	1.91	2.12	2.53	3.10	4.00	4.91	5.92	8.30
8	1.96	2.21	2.68	3.32	4.35	5.39	6.55	9.26
9	2.02	2.30	2.82	3.55	4.70	5.87	7.17	10.22
10	2.07	2.38	2.97	3.78	5.05	6.35	7.79	11.18
11	2.13	2.47	3.11	4.00	5.40	6.83	8.42	12.14
12	2.19	2.56	3.25	4.22	5.75	7.30	9.03	13.09
13	2.24	2.64	3.40	4.44	6.10	7.78	9.65	14.03
14	2.28	2.69	3.48	4.56	6.27	8.02	9.96	14.50
15	2.32	2.75	3.55	4.67	6.44	8.24	10.24	14.94
16	2.35	2.79	3.63	4.78	6.60	8.45	10.52	15.35
17	2.39	2.84	3.70	4.88	6.75	8.66	10.77	15.74
18	2.42	2.89	3.76	4.98	6.90	8.85	11.02	16.11
19	2.46	2.93	3.83	5.07	7.03	9.03	11.25	16.45
20	2.49	2.98	3.89	5.16	7.16	9.20	11.47	16.79

ZONE CHART

STATE	ZONE	STATE	ZONE
Alaska	8	Montana	8
California	8	Nevada	8
Canal Zone	8	New Hampshire	6
Canton Island	8	New York	6
Caroline Islands	8	New Mexico	7
Connecticut	6	Oregon	8
Delaware	5	Puerto Rico	6
District of Columbia	5	Rhode Island	6
Guam	8	Samoa (American)	8
Hawaii	8	South Dakota	7
Idaho	8	Tennessee	5
Kentucky	5	Utah	8
Louisiana	5	Vermont	6
Mariana Islands	8	Virgin Islands	6
Marshall Islands	8	Virginia	5
Maryland	5	Wake Island	8
Massachusetts	6	Washington	8
Minnesota	7	West Virginia	5
Mississippi	5		

Refer to the appropriate charts above and determine the amount of postage required for each of the following problems.

7. Ted Fox mailed the following items via parcel post for LaStrada Enterprises. Using the tables, determine the postage for each item and the total postage for all the pieces.

a. A 20-pound package to Kentucky.
b. A $13\frac{3}{4}$-pound package to Washington.
c. A 4.5-pound package to New Mexico.
d. A package to Massachusetts weighing 11 pounds 6 ounces.
e. Total postage.

8. Susan Blair mailed the following items by parcel post. Determine the postage for each package and the total postage for all the pieces.

a. A 1 pound 11 ounce package to a local merchant.
b. A 7 pound 15 ounce package to a customer in Zone 2.
c. A 17 pound $5\frac{1}{2}$ ounce parcel to American Samoa.
d. A 2 pound 1 ounce parcel to Wilmington, Delaware.
e. The total postage.

9. Winchester Gift Distributors mailed five packages by fourth class mail. Determine the total postage for these packages: 5 pounds, 2 ounces to San Juan, Puerto Rico; 4 pounds 15 ounces to Boise, Idaho; 11 pounds to Baltimore, Maryland; 2 pounds 9 ounces to Wayzata, Minnesota; 15 pounds 5 ounces to Honolulu, Hawaii.

ANSWERS

7. **a.** ________
b. ________
c. ________
d. ________
e. ________

8. **a.** ________
b. ________
c. ________
d. ________
e. ________

9. ________

Material sent by First-Class Letter Mail, or Next Day Express Mail Service, is charged postage according to the appropriate rate. Other services offered, such as insurance, registered and certified mail, and return receipt, are all charges added on top of the regular postage charge. The charts below are examples of the rates charged for some of these other services.

Example: How much would it cost to mail a first-class letter weighing $2\frac{3}{4}$ ounces?

Solution: Refer to the First-Class Letter Rate schedule. Since the letter weighs more than 2 ounces, and less than 3 ounces, the postage would be $0.65.

Example: How much would it cost to mail a 1 pound package by Express Mail Service, insured for $145.?

Solution: Express Mail, more than 8 ounces, but less than 2 pounds, requires postage of $12.00. The insurance fee for a value of more than $100, but less than $150, is $1.90. The total postage would be

$$\$12.00 + \$1.90 = \$13.90.$$

FIRST-CLASS

LETTER RATES:

1st ounce	$0.25
Each additional ounce	0.20

For pieces not exceeding (oz.)	*The Rate Is*	*For pieces not exceeding (oz.)*	*The Rate Is*
1	$0.25	7	$1.45
2	0.45	8	1.65
3	0.65	9	1.85
4	0.85	10	2.05
5	1.05	11	2.25
6	1.25		

FOR PIECES OVER 11 OUNCES, SEE PRIORITY MAIL RATES

Presort rates	Consult Postmaster
Business reply mail	Consult Postmaster

CARD RATES:

Single postal cards sold by the post office	$0.15 each
Double postal cards sold by the post office	0.30 ($0.15 each half)
Single post cards	0.15 each
Double post cards (reply-half of double post card does not have to bear postage when originally mailed)	$0.30 ($0.15 each half)

Note To qualify for card rates, a card may not be larger than 4¼ by 6 inches, nor smaller than 3½ by 5 inches. The thickness must be uniform and not less than 0.007 of an inch

EXPRESS MAIL.

NEXT DAY SERVICE

AN OVERNIGHT DELIVERY SERVICE THAT'S FAST, RELIABLE, CONVENIENT AND ECONOMICAL

Express Mail Service is available 7 days a week, 365 days a year (at no additional charge) for mailable items up to 70 pounds in weight and 108 inches in combined length and girth

Flat rates for Post Office to Addressee service letter rate (up to 8 ounces) $8.75 up to 2 lbs. $12.00 over 2 lbs and up to 5 lbs $15.25 consult Postmaster for rates for items exceeding 5 lbs up to 70 lbs

Service features include Noon delivery between major business markets merchandise and document reconstruction insurance Express Mail shipping containers shipment receipt optional return receipt service optional COD service waiver of signature option collection boxes optional pickup service

Consult Postmaster or account representative for additional information on other Express Mail services (same day airport, custom designed, military and international) and a copy of your local Express Mail network directory

The Postal Service will refund, upon application to the originating office the postage for any Express Mail shipments not meeting the service standard except for those delayed by strike or work stoppage

SPECIAL SERVICES—DOMESTIC MAIL ONLY

INSURANCE
For Coverage Against Loss or Damage

Fees (in addition to postage)

Liability	*Fee*
$ 0.01 to $ 50.00	$0.70
50.01 to 100.00	1.50
100.01 to 150.00	1.90
150.01 to 200.00	2.20
200.01 to 300.00	3.15
300.01 to 400.00	4.30
400.01 to 500.00	5.00

REGISTRY
For Maximum Protection and Security

Value	*Fees in addition to postage*	
	For articles covered by Postal Insurance	*For articles not covered by Postal Insurance*
$0.01 to 100.00	$4.50	$4.40
$100.01 to 500.00	4.85	4.70
500.01 to 1,000.00	5.25	5.05
For higher values, consult Postmaster		

SPECIAL DELIVERY

(In addition to required postage)

Class of Mail	*Weight*		
	Not more than 2 pounds	*More than 2 pounds but not more than 10 pounds*	*More than 10 pounds*
First Class	$5.35	$5.75	$7.25
All other classes	5.65	6.50	8.10

ADDITIONAL SERVICES

CERTIFIED MAIL—Fee (in addition to postage)	$0.85
CERTIFICATE OF MAILING—Fee (in addition to postage) (For Bulk mailings and Firm mailing books, see Postmaster)	$0.45
RESTRICTED DELIVERY (for Insured*, Certified, and Registered Mail)	$2.00
RETURN RECEIPT (with Insured*, Certified, and Registered Mail)	
Requested at time of mailing:	
Showing to whom and when delivered	$0.90
Showing to whom, when, and address where delivered	1.20
Requested after mailing:	
Showing to whom and when delivered	$5.00
*Not available for mail insured for $50 or less	
RETURN RECEIPT FOR MERCHANDISE (without another special service)	
Showing to whom and when delivered	$1.00
Showing to whom, when, and where delivered	1.35

10. The five packages shipped by Winchester Gift Distributors in problem 9 were insured for the following amounts: $179; $212; $309; $51; and $399. What would the total postage be for mailing these packages?

ANSWERS

10. __________

11. Brenda Chang mailed a letter weighing $3\frac{1}{2}$ ounces to a cousin in San Francisco. It was mailed first–class, certified, return receipt requested. What was the total postage for this mailing?

12. Betty Hahn sent a package of repair parts to Henry Fromkin's Taxi Service. The package weighed 4 pounds 14 ounces, and was insured for $150. What was the total postage paid by Betty Hahn?

13. Renee Schmeltz mailed her grandfather's gold pocket watch to Hilltop Jewelers in Overland Park, Kansas. The watch was valued at $385. The package weighed $8\frac{1}{2}$ ounces, and was sent first-class, registered, insured, return receipt requested. What was the total amount of postage which she paid?

14. Peter DeGroot returned a mantle clock to the factory in Danbury, Connecticut. The clock weighed 18 pounds, 8 ounces, and was shipped fourth class, special delivery, insured for $495. What is the total amount of postage paid to mail this package?

15. Helmsley Laboratories mailed a collection specimen to a processing laboratory located in Fourth Class Zone 3. The package weighed 1 pound, $11\frac{1}{2}$ ounces, and was mailed with special handling. What was the total amount of postage paid?

16. Blanche Baker returned a $1,000 registered bond to Meridian Assets Management. She was instructed to mail it first-class, special delivery, registered, return receipt requested, but not insured. The envelope weighed $1\frac{1}{2}$ ounces. What was the total amount of postage which she paid?

17. Peter Metz returned a damaged book to the publisher who was located in Zone 2. He mailed it regular fourth class, but requested a return receipt showing to whom, when, and where it was delivered. The package weighed 3 pounds 7 ounces. What was the amount of postage paid?

ANSWERS

11. ____________

12. ____________

13. ____________

14. ____________

15. ____________

16. ____________

17. ____________

NAME DATE

SKILL BUILDER — Reading Graphs — 16B

LINE GRAPHS A **graph** is a visual means of displaying numerical information or data. Graphs are generally less accurate than tables, but they can be effectively used to show trends or comparisons. A **line graph,** or **polygon,** is a form of graph in which information is plotted as points on horizontal and vertical scales. These points are then connected with a line. More than one set of data or information can be shown on a single line graph. The following line graph shows the sales in one week for three shifts of the clothing department of Bud's Discount House. This graph was constructed by locating, or plotting, the points representing sales on the vertical scale, and the points for each day on the horizontal scale. Each shift was plotted separately, and the points for each shift were then connected. A different type of line was used for each shift.

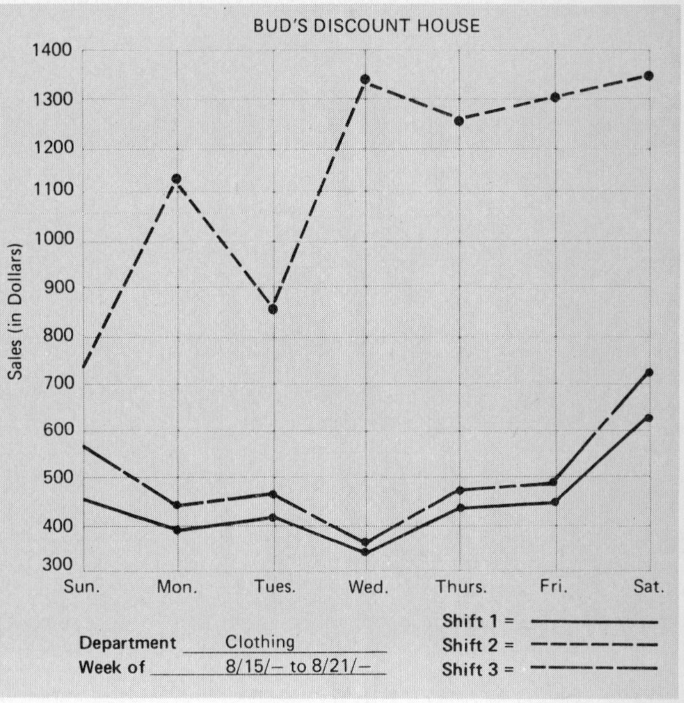

1. Answer the following questions using the information shown on the line graph above.

a. What was the approximate amount of sales on Wednesday for shift 2?

b. What was the approximate difference in sales between shift 1 and shift 3 on Saturday?

c. Which shift had the greatest amount of sales on Tuesday?

d. For how many days did shift 2 have sales above $1,000?

e. Which shift generally has the greatest amount of sales?

f. Which shift generally has the least amount of sales?

ANSWERS

1. a. ____________

b. ____________

c. ____________

d. ____________

e. ____________

f. ____________

BAR GRAPHS A **histogram** is a graph which is useful for showing differences between categories. It consists of perpendicular scales, with bars drawn to represent the amounts. The following histogram shows the results of a survey of the ages of the first 50 customers to make a purchase at the Sportsway Athletic Supply Store on a single day. The horizontal scale gives seven age group ranges. The vertical scale gives the number of customers in each age group. The results of the survey are illustrated by the bars drawn on the graph. The top of each bar indicates the number of persons in each age group.

Example: How many customers are in the 30–34 year age group?

Solution: Locate the 30–34 year age group on the horizontal scale. The height of this bar represents the number of customers in this age group. Read across from the top of this bar to the vertical scale on the left. There were 6 customers in this age group.

A **bar graph** is similar to a histogram, except that the bars are separated by space. This form of graph is often used to compare data from one period to another. Bar graphs can be drawn either horizontally or vertically, and can present data from more than one period. Bar graphs are read in the same manner as histograms. The following bar graph compares sales this year with sales for last year in six departments of Bud's Discount House.

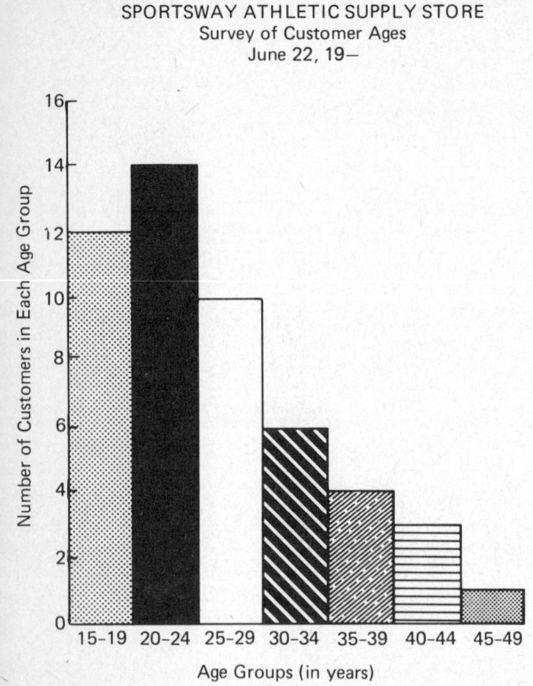

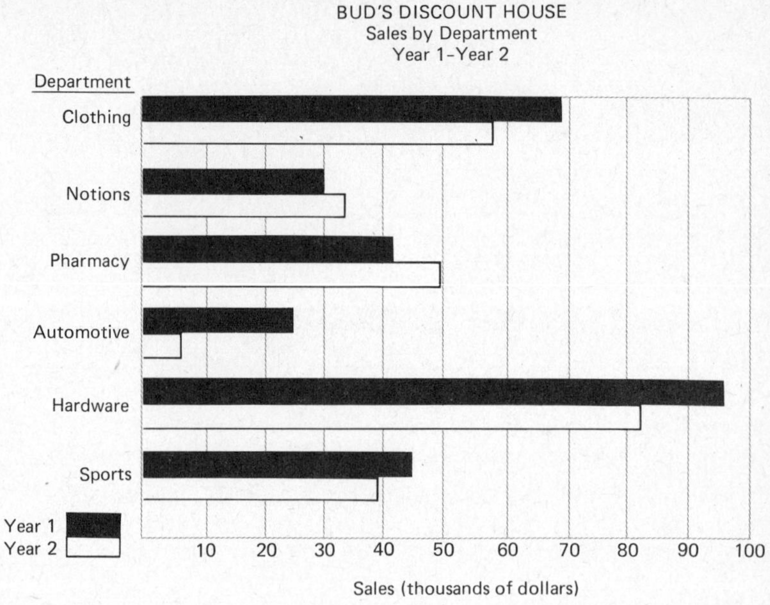

2. Use the histogram above to answer the following questions.

a. Which age group has 10 customers?

b. How many customers are in the 35–39 year age group?

c. Which age group had the most customers?

d. Which age group had the fewest customers?

e. How many customers were between 30 and 49 years of age?

ANSWERS

2. a. ______________

b. ______________

c. ______________

d. ______________

e. ______________

3. Use the graph on page 70 to answer the following questions.

a. What was the approximate amount of sales in the notions department for year 1?

b. Which departments had sales over $50,000 in year 1?

c. Approximately how much did automotive sales decrease from year 1 to year 2?

d. Which departments had higher sales in year 1 than in year 2?

e. What is the approximate amount of the total sales in year 1 for the Clothing and Sports Departments combined?

ANSWERS

3. a. __________

b. __________

c. __________

d. __________

e. __________

CIRCLE GRAPHS A **circle graph** is an effective way to show how individual parts relate to the whole. For example, in the circle graph below, the entire circle represents one dollar of federal government income, or 100 percent. The total income is broken down into different categories: income tax, FICA tax, corporate income tax, and so on. Each of these categories is displayed on a portion of the circle that represents that portion of the income. For example, income tax accounts for 38 cents of every dollar of income. This is equivalent to 38 percent.

$$\frac{\$0.38}{\$1.00} = \frac{38}{100} = 38\%$$

WHERE THE FEDERAL GOVERNMENT GETS ITS MONEY

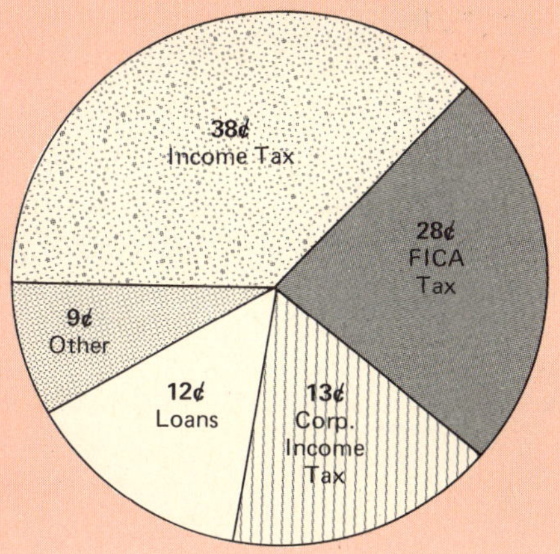

1 Dollar

4. Answer the following questions using the circle graph above.

a. How many cents of each dollar of federal income come from corporate income tax?

b. What percent of federal income is obtained from corporate income tax?

c. What percent of federal income is obtained from taxes of all types?

d. What percent of federal income is obtained from sources other than taxes?

ANSWERS

4. a. __________

b. __________

c. __________

d. __________

5. Answer the following questions using the circle graph shown below.

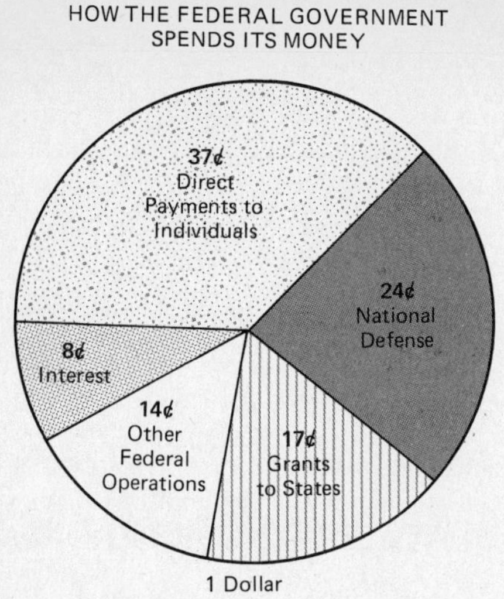

a. What percent of the federal budget is spent on interest payments?
b. What percent of the federal budget is *not* spent on national defense?
c. What percent of the federal budget is returned directly to the states?
d. What percent of the federal budget is returned directly to the states and to individuals?

6. Answer the following questions using the circle graph shown below.

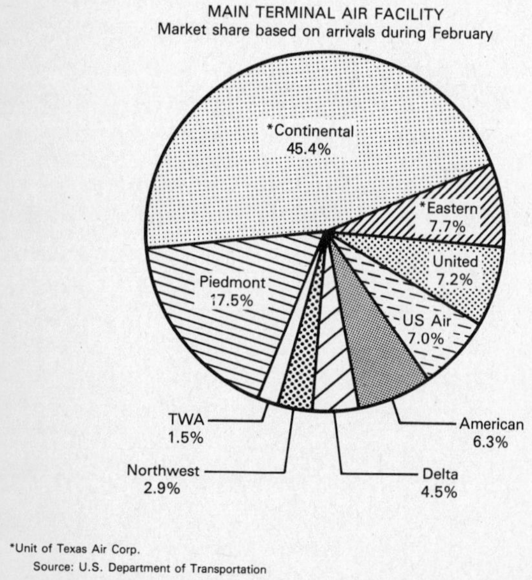

a. Which airline had the largest market share of arrivals?
b. Which airline had the smallest market share of arrivals?
c. Which airline had the second largest market share of arrivals?
d. What percent of total market share of arrivals did Continental and Eastern have combined?

ANSWERS

5. a. ____________
b. ____________
c. ____________
d. ____________

6. a. ____________
b. ____________
c. ____________
d. ____________

NAME DATE

SKILL BUILDER — The Percentage Formula — 17A

RENAMING PERCENTS AND DECIMAL FRACTIONS Decimal fractions can be expressed as fractions with denominators of 100, 1,000, 10,000, and so on; they can also be expressed as percents. **Percent** means per hundred. To rename a decimal fraction as a percent, move the decimal point two places *to the right* and add the percent sign. To rename a percent as a decimal fraction, move the decimal point two places *to the left* and remove the percent sign.

0.45 = 0.45.% 0.333 = 0.33.3%

45% = 0.45. 33.3% = 0.33.3

To rename a percent as a common fraction, first express the percent as a decimal fraction. Then write the decimal fraction as a common fraction, and reduce it to simplest terms.

$$8\tfrac{3}{4}\% = 0.0875 = \frac{875}{10{,}000} = \frac{7}{80}$$

RENAMING COMMON FRACTIONS To rename a common fraction as a decimal fraction, divide the numerator by the denominator. If the fraction does not divide evenly, round off the answer.

$\frac{1}{4} = 0.25$ $\frac{3}{10} = 0.30$

$\frac{5}{8} = 0.625$ $1\frac{1}{8} = 1.125$

Rename each common fraction as (a) a decimal fraction (rounded off to the fourth decimal place where necessary) and then to (b) a percent.

	a.	b.		a.	b.		a.	b.
1. $\frac{1}{2}$ =	______ =	______	2. $\frac{1}{5}$ =	______ =	______	3. $\frac{3}{8}$ =	______ =	______
4. $\frac{1}{8}$ =	______ =	______	5. $\frac{1}{3}$ =	______ =	______	6. $\frac{4}{5}$ =	______ =	______
7. $\frac{1}{10}$ =	______ =	______	8. $\frac{7}{8}$ =	______ =	______	9. $\frac{1}{6}$ =	______ =	______
10. $\frac{1}{9}$ =	______ =	______	11. $1\frac{3}{8}$ =	______ =	______	12. $\frac{2}{3}$ =	______ =	______
13. $\frac{3}{5}$ =	______ =	______	14. $\frac{1}{12}$ =	______ =	______	15. $\frac{1}{16}$ =	______ =	______

Rename each percent as a common fraction. Reduce to lowest terms, where necessary.

16. 25% = ______	17. 35% = ______	18. 16% = ______	19. 7% = ______
20. 45% = ______	21. $33\frac{1}{3}\%$ = ______	22. 15% = ______	23. $62\frac{1}{2}\%$ = ______
24. $6\frac{1}{4}\%$ = ______	25. 225% = ______	26. $83\frac{1}{3}\%$ = ______	27. $37\frac{1}{2}\%$ = ______
28. $2\frac{1}{4}\%$ = ______	29. $\frac{1}{4}\%$ = ______	30. 375% = ______	31. $87\frac{1}{2}\%$ = ______

BASE × RATE = PERCENTAGE FORMULA A percent is a **rate.** When a rate is applied to an amount (for example, 50% of 300), the result is a **percentage.** The formula *Base × Rate = Percentage* can be used to find the percentage.

Example: What is 30% of $615?

Solution: *Base × Rate = Percentage*
$615 × 0.30 = $184.50

Example: What is $62\frac{1}{2}$% of 120?

Solution: $62\frac{1}{2}$% = 0.625

Base × Rate = Percentage
120 × 0.625 = 75

Compute the percentage in the following problems using the formula *Base × Rate = Percentage (B × R = P).* Use the aliquot part equivalent for the rate (percent) whenever it will help solve the problem.

32. 8% of $500

33. 5% of $42.80

34. 25% of $5,800

35. 2% of 90

36. 72% of 613

37. $8\frac{1}{3}$% of 288

38. $12\frac{1}{2}$% of $8,010

39. $2\frac{1}{2}$% of $340

40. $16\frac{2}{3}$% of 264

41. Thomas Jameson was paid a commission of 5 percent on sales totalling $78,000 last month. How much did he earn for the month?

42. Albert Graham received an $8\frac{1}{3}$ percent increase in his $25,848 annual salary.
a. What was the total amount of his increase?
b. How much did his monthly salary increase?
c. What is his new annual salary?

43. Emma Channing, sales manager for Queens' Cosmetics, is projecting an $11\frac{1}{9}$ percent increase in sales for the next quarter. Sales for this quarter were $412,893.
a. What is the expected amount of increase for the next quarter's sales?
b. If the increase is attained, what will total sales be for the next quarter?

44. Ellen Marcus, marketing manager for Queens' Cosmetics, conducted a market survey and determined that 50.1 percent of the 35,000 people questioned recognized at least one product produced by Queens' Cosmetics. How many people surveyed knew about their products?

ANSWERS

32. ____________
33. ____________
34. ____________
35. ____________
36. ____________
37. ____________
38. ____________
39. ____________
40. ____________
41. ____________
42. a. ____________
b. ____________
c. ____________
43. a. ____________
b. ____________
44. ____________

NAME DATE

SKILL BUILDER 17B

Computing the Rate, Base, Increase, and Decrease

The basic percentage formula can be rewritten to find either the base or the rate.

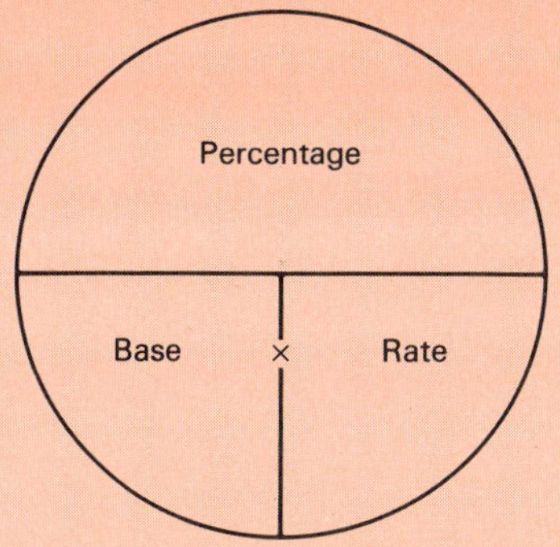

BASE × RATE = PERCENTAGE
B × R = P

Place a finger over the word representing the unknown element in the formula. The remaining portions of the chart indicate what operation is necessary to find the unknown. For example, what is 30% of 340? Since the percentage is the unknown, multiply the base times the rate.

$$B \times R = P$$
$$340 \times 0.30 = 102$$

If the base is the unknown, divide the percentage by the rate. For example, 102 is 30 percent of what number? The percentage (102) and the rate (30%) are both known.

$$P \div R = B$$
$$102 \div 0.30 = 340$$

If the rate is the unknown, divide the percentage by the base. For example, what percent of 340 is 102? The percentage (102) and the base (340) are both known.

$$P \div B = R$$
$$102 \div 340 = 0.30 = 30\%$$

Find the base in each of the following problems. Remember to rename the percent as a decimal fraction, rounding off the decimal to 4 places where necessary.

1. 25% of $__?__ = $144 ________

2. 30% of $__?__ = $21.90 ________

3. 40% of $__?__ = $75.60 ________

4. $12\frac{1}{2}$% of $__?__ = $42 ________

5. 8% of __?__ = 4.96 ________

6. $16\frac{2}{3}$% of $__?__ = $264 ________

7. $37\frac{1}{2}$% of __?__ = 18 ________

8. $\frac{1}{2}$% of $__?__ = $10 ________

9. $62\frac{1}{2}$% of $__?__ = $55 ________

10. $8\frac{1}{3}$% of $__?__ = $9 ________

Find the rate, to the nearest hundredth, where necessary, in each of the following problems.

11. $18 is what percent of $72? ________

12. What percent of 128 is 3.84? ________

13. $78 is what percent of $156? ________

14. $13.50 is what percent of $162? ________

15. 64 is what percent of 192? ________

16. __?__% of $60 is $6 ________

17. ___?___% of 150 = 30 __________

18. ___?___% of 63 = $7\frac{7}{8}$ __________

19. ___?___% of \$64 = \$56 __________

20. ___?___% of \$114 = \$38 __________

INCREASE Many percentage problems are concerned with an increase or decrease in amount. An **increase** problem is one in which the new amount (percentage) is *larger* than the original amount (base). *Adding* 100% (representing the base) to the **rate of increase** results in a new rate representing the new amount (percentage). When the base is multiplied by this new rate, the resulting product will be the new amount.

Example: The price of coffee has just increased by 20 percent from \$2.15 a pound. What is the increased price?

Solution:

Base	×	*Rate*		=	*Percentage*
Original Amount	× (*100%* +	*Rate of Increase*)		=	*New Larger Amount*
\$2.15	× (100% +	20%	)	=	?
\$2.15	×	1.20		=	\$2.58

Find the percentage in each problem.

21. 120 increased by 10% __________

22. 56 increased by 25% __________

23. \$6.80 increased by 20% __________

24. 50 increased by 100% __________

When the percentage and the rate of increase are known, the base is found by dividing the percentage by 100% plus the rate of increase.

Example: Coffee is now selling at \$2.58 per pound, which is 20 percent greater than its earlier price. What was the price of coffee before the increase?

Solution: The base is unknown. Divide the percentage (\$2.58) by the rate (100% + 20% increase) to find the original price.

Percentage	÷	*Rate*		=	*Base*
New Larger Amount	÷ (*100%* +	*Rate of Increase*)		=	*Original Amount*
\$2.58	÷ (100% +	20%	)	=	?
\$2.58	÷	1.20		=	\$2.15

Check:
\$2.15 × 0.20 = \$0.43   \$2.15 + \$0.43 = \$2.58

Find the base in each problem.

25. __________ × 1.25 = 60

26. __________ × 1.6 = 80

27. __________ × 1.20 = 240

28. __________ × 2.00 = 356

29. __________ increased by 20% = 120

30. __________ increased by 60% = 32

31. __________ increased by $12\frac{1}{2}\%$ = 99

32. __________ increased by 100% = 78

DECREASE With **decrease** problems, the percentage, the new amount, is always *less* than the base. Subtracting the **rate of decrease** from 100% (representing the base) results in a new rate. When the base is multiplied by this new rate, the resulting product will be the new amount (percentage).

Example: An electronic game console was originally priced at $352. The price is to be reduced by 25 percent. What will the new (reduced) price be?

Solution:

Base	×	*Rate*		=	*Percentage*
Original Amount	×	*(100%* −	*Rate of Decrease)*	=	*New Lesser Amount*
$352	×	(100% −	25%)	=	?
$352	×	0.75		=	$264

Find the percentage in each of the following decrease problems. Round off percents to 4 decimal places.

33. 40 decreased by 25% = __________ 34. $120 reduced by $33\frac{1}{3}$% = __________

35. $480 reduced by 16% = __________ 36. 978 reduced by 50% = __________

37. 58 reduced by $37\frac{1}{2}$% = __________ 38. $129 reduced by $16\frac{2}{3}$% = __________

When the percentage and the rate of decrease are known, the base is found by dividing the percentage by 100% minus the rate of decrease.

Example: An electronic game console is sale priced at $264, which is a 25 percent reduction from the original price. What was the original price?

Solution:

Percentage	÷	*Rate*		=	*Base*
New Lesser Amount	÷	*(100%* −	*Rate of Decrease)*	=	*Original Amount*
$264	÷	(100% −	25%)	=	?
$264	÷	0.75		=	$352

Check:

$352 × 0.25 = $88; $352 − $88 = $264

Find the base in each decrease problem below. Round off percents to 4 decimal places.

39. __________ × 0.78 = 78 40. __________ × 0.625 = 640

41. __________ × 0.45 = 33.75 42. __________ × 0.50 = 1,025

43. __________ decreased by 29% = $177.50 44. __________ decreased by 15% = 85

45. __________ decreased by $8\frac{1}{3}$% = $44 46. __________ decreased by 60% = 48

47. __________ decreased by $33\frac{1}{3}$% = 950 48. __________ decreased by 62.5% = 642

In the following problems, round off percents to 2 decimal places, where necessary.

49. The sale price of Sun Screen Skin Lotion is \$4 after a 20 percent discount. What was the original price?

50. The new price of a Speed-King moped is \$678 after a 13 percent increase. What was the original price?

51. Last Sunday evening Quick-Serve had 656 customers. This was 18 percent fewer customers than the previous week. How many customers were there the previous Sunday evening?

52. Orbit Sales inadvertently included 5 percent sales tax in a bill to a tax exempt organization. The bill showed a total of \$247.80, which included the 5 percent sales tax. What is the amount of tax which must be deducted to correct this over-billing?

53. Membership in the Side Winder Racquet Club has dropped by $8\frac{1}{4}$ percent, according to Rene Ping, the manager. This year's membership is 1,925 adults and children. What was last year's membership? Round off your final answer to the nearest whole unit.

54. A starter motor is priced at \$75, with a markup of 25 percent of cost. What is the cost for the starter?

55. Betty Ong receives a 15 percent bonus on each order she obtains. If Betty received a \$975 bonus on one order, what was the amount of the order?

56. Jo-Ellen DeNarzo sold a house for \$165,000, including the land. This gave her a 20 percent profit over the cost of the land and the house.

a. How much was her profit?

b. If the land cost \$34,375, what percent of the total cost did the cost of the house represent?

57. Peter Murphy made a partial payment of \$262.50 on an overdue bill. This payment included a 5 percent penalty charge on the payment. If the payment, before the penalty, was 25 percent of what he owed, how much did he owe?

58. Pearl Pewter Products laid off 15 percent of its total work force. If 51 workers remained, what was the total work force before the layoff?

59. The local tax rate was increased by $5\frac{1}{2}$ percent to a rate of \$6.963 of every \$100. What was the tax rate prior to the increase?

60. Burger Buster had to increase their hourly wage rate to \$5.65 per hour, in order to get people to work for them. This rate is 13% higher than the prevailing minimum hourly wage rate being paid in the area. What is the prevailing minimum hourly wage rate?

ANSWERS

49. __________

50. __________

51. __________

52. __________

53. __________

54. __________

55. __________

56. a. __________

b. __________

57. __________

58. __________

59. __________

60. __________

NAME ____________ DATE ____________

SKILL BUILDER 18A

Computing Sales Commissions

COMMISSIONS Many people do not work for an hourly wage or a weekly or monthly salary. Rather, they receive a commission. The most common example of a person who receives a commission is a salesperson. Sheila Collins works for the Graham Decorators. She receives a 6 percent commission on all sales that she makes. During the past week, Sheila sold $8,200 worth of furniture. Her commission would be $492.

$8,200	Sales
×0.06	Commission rate
$ 492	Commission

Some salespeople receive a salary plus a commission. Marge Tyler sells furniture for Emmett Designs. She receives a weekly salary of $100 plus an additional 3 percent commission on all sales. Last week, Marge sold $9,600 worth of furniture. Her salary plus commission would be $388.

$9,600	Sales	$288	Commission
×0.03	Commission rate	+100	Salary
$ 288	Commission	$388	Total earnings

Some salespersons earn a base salary and a commission only on the amount that their sales exceed a certain figure or quota. For example, Tonya Gibson earns a base salary of $250 per week and a percentage commission of 5% on all sales over $2,500. Tonya's sales for the past week were $10,800.

$10,800	Sales for week	$250	Base salary
−2,500	Min. Quota	+415	Commission
$ 8,300	Sales over $2,500	$665	Total Earnings

$ 8,300	
×0.05	Commission Rate
$ 415	Commission

1. Find the commissions for these salespeople based on their weekly sales.

	SALESPERSON	RATE OF COMMISSION	WEEKLY SALES	COMMISSION
a.	Martin Beck	5%	$8,000	________
b.	Jack Longacre	6%	$7,800	________
c.	Jane Hayes	4%	$9,600	________
d.	Alice Bittmore	7%	$7,100	________
e.	Carl Covell	8%	$8,540	________

2. Find the total of the base salary plus commission for each salesperson based on weekly sales.

	SALESPERSON	BASE SALARY	RATE OF COMMISSION	WEEKLY SALES	SALARY PLUS COMMISSION
a.	John Bean	$100	5%	$5,500	________
b.	Randy Beasley	100	6%	4,000	________
c.	Marge Champion	150	6%	3,800	________
d.	Hilary Dawson	75	8%	4,440	________
e.	Dawn Gargan	175	7%	4,300	________

3. These salespersons receive a base salary of $125 a week and a commission of 6 percent on all sales over $1,000. Compute the total earnings of each salesperson.

	SALESPERSON	WEEKLY SALES	AMOUNT OF COMMISSION	TOTAL EARNINGS
a.	Mike Dawes	$ 6,000.	________	________
b.	Pat Hunt	5,580.	________	________
c.	Lois Lipfield	5,700.	________	________
d.	Ruth Moore	14,480.	________	________
e.	Jim Roberts	9,000.	________	________

Some businesses base their commissions on a sliding scale. For instance, salespersons at Tern Products Inc. earn a 5 percent commission on all sales up to and including $1,000; a 7 percent commission on sales from $1,001 up to and including $2,000; and a 10 percent commission on all sales of $2,001 or more.

For example, Wallace Redford had sales of $5,200 one week. What are his total earnings for the week?

Sales ×	*Commission Rates*	=	*Commission*
$1,000 ×	0.05	=	$ 50
1,000 ×	0.07	=	70
3,200 ×	0.10	=	320
	Total	=	$440

Salespersons who work for a sliding scale commission may or may not receive a base salary in addition to their commission.

4. Find the total earnings for each Tern Products Inc. salesperson. The commission paid to each is based on the sliding scale explained above.

TERN PRODUCTS INC.

Weekly Earnings Report
May 23, 19—

SALESPERSON	TOTAL SALES	AMOUNT OF COMMISSION	BASE SALARY	TOTAL EARNINGS
Bassett, M.	$5,200	________	$ 75	________
Copeland, J.	5,000	________	125	________
DelTorto, V.	5,500	________	100	________
Englert, T.	4,600	________	125	________
Fusco, C.	5,800	________	75	________
Franklin, H.	6,100	________	100	________
Handley, E.	5,140	________	125	________
Montez, W.	5,480	________	100	________
Oroz, J.	6,120	________	125	________
Pappas, N.	7,600	________	100	________
Preston, O.	6,800	________	125	________
Restic, V.	4,400	________	100	________
Savage, K.	6,200	________	100	________
Truax, P.	3,940	________	75	________
Weston, A.	6,400	________	100	________
Zeramba, L.	3,440	________	100	________
	Totals	________	________	________

NAME DATE

SKILL BUILDER 18B

Computing Agents' Commissions

AGENTS In today's complex business world, many persons do not have the necessary knowledge, skills, or time needed to handle their business affairs. These people often use the service of agents. The **agent** is a financial expert who handles other people's business affairs. The person who is represented by the agent is the **client.** Agents may be paid a base salary; most, however, work on a commission plan.

A common type of agent is one who represents a professional athlete. The agent negotiates the player's contract and receives a percentage (frequently 10 percent) of the negotiated figure. In addition to the commission earned on the player's contract, the agent may also earn a commission for other business dealings arranged for the client, such as speaking engagements, public appearances, television commercials, magazine advertisements, and so on.

Example: Marion Castello, a real estate agent, earned a 10 percent commission for selling a $500,000 building. What commission did she earn on this sale?

Solution:

Commission	=	*Sales Amount*	×	*Rate of Commission*
?	=	$500,000	×	10%
?	=	$ 50,000		

1. Agents negotiated the contracts listed below for professional athletes. The negotiated annual salary for each athlete is shown along with the commission rate earned by the agent. The agents also receive a percentage from other sources, such as speaking engagements, public appearances, television commercials, and magazine advertisements. Find the total commission earned by each agent.

AGENT	NEGOTIATED CONTRACT	COMMISSION RATE	COMMISSION EARNED	OTHER SOURCES	COMMISSION RATE	COMMISSION EARNED	TOTAL COMMISSION
B. Consorno	$ 85,000	10%	________	$ 3,000	3%	________	________
G. Donofrio	100,000	10%	________	7,000	3%	________	________
H. Fredericks	50,000	10%	________	1,800	3%	________	________
M. Hernandez	130,000	10%	________	6,300	4%	________	________
P. Jablonski	250,000	12%	________	7,500	3%	________	________
O. Landry	190,000	8%	________	7,000	5%	________	________
R. Peterman	450,000	10%	________	12,500	4%	________	________
M. Sorenson	175,000	8%	________	5,600	5%	________	________
T. Torrez	500,000	12%	________	18,500	6%	________	________
W. Victor	90,000	10%	________	5,000	4%	________	________
H. Yarborough	235,000	8%	________	6,300	3%	________	________

2. Complete these sales agents' records.

FAWN'S FASHIONS

SALES AGENT'S RECORD — Oct. 18, 19—

NAME: M. Richard — NO. 54

DATE	GROSS SALES	RETURNS	TOTAL NET SALES
14	$1,835.40	$210.26	________
15	1,550.50	23.48	________
16	1,470.98	115.75	________
17	2,005.25	–0–	________
18	1,450.32	154.62	________
	________	________	________

Less sales tax 5% ________

Total for commission ________

Commission at $4\frac{3}{4}$% ________

FAWN'S FASHIONS

SALES AGENT'S RECORD — Oct. 18, 19—

NAME: T. Dulong — NO. 55

DATE	GROSS SALES	RETURNS	TOTAL NET SALES
14	$2,580.00	$ 45.50	________
15	2,050.55	115.80	________
16	2,187.23	–0–	________
17	2,793.18	231.00	________
18	3,050.50	177.65	________
	________	________	________

Less sales tax 5% ________

Total for commission ________

Commission at $5\frac{3}{4}$% ________

3. Fawn's Fashions pays its sales agents an hourly wage plus a $3\frac{1}{2}$ percent commission for the first 60 days of their employment. Complete this sales record.

FAWN'S FASHIONS

SALES AGENT'S RECORD — Oct. 18, 19—

NAME: B. Chase — NO. 235

DATE	HOURS	GROSS SALES	RETURNS	TOTAL NET SALES
14	8	$ 450.00	–0–	________
15	7	1,100.45	$135.65	________
16	8	874.35	26.50	________
17	$7\frac{1}{2}$	1,350.24	–0–	________
18	8	937.65	85.65	________
		________	________	________

Less sales tax 5% ________

Total for commission ________

Commission at $3\frac{1}{2}$% ________

________ Hours @ $4.10 an hr. ________

Total earnings ________

4. The manager of Fawn's Fashions is paid $500 a week plus 5% of the commissions earned by the sales agents. How much did Jerry Rosen earn for the week of Oct. 18?

FAWN'S FASHIONS

MANAGER'S REPORT

LOCATION: Ledgewood — WEEK OF 10/18/—

SALES AGENT	COMMISSION EARNED
Dulong, T.	$________
Richard, M.	$________
Chase, B.	$________
Weekly Total	$________
Manager's Commission @ 5%	$________
Manager's Weekly Pay	$________
Total earnings	$________

NAME DATE

SKILL BUILDER 19A

Solving Word Problems

A key to solving word problems is knowing when to add, subtract, multiply, or divide. Often key words in the problem will indicate which operations are required. For example, *of, as much as, as great as,* and *as large as,* usually indicate multiplication. *For each, per,* and *average* often indicate division. *Increase, plus, more, total, sum, larger,* and *greater* usually indicate addition. *Decrease, less, difference,* and *diminished,* often indicate subtraction. The word *what* indicates the unknown factor; *is* indicates equals. Examining these key words will help in expressing a word problem as a number problem.

RULES FOR SOLVING WORD PROBLEMS Read the problem carefully, more than once if necessary. Then follow these steps.

1. List the known and unknown factors.
2. Find the key words indicating operation.
3. Write a simple formula using the factors and operation found in steps 1 and 2.
4. Perform the operations indicated.
5. Check your answer.

Example: Elbert Products spent $1,800 on a holiday party for their 40 employees. What was the cost of the party for each employee?

Solution:

1. *What are the known factors?*
   Cost of party—$1,800
   Number of employees—40
   What is the unknown factor? Cost for each employee
2. *Key words: for each* indicate division
3. $1,800 ÷ 40 = ?
4. $1,800 ÷ 40 = $45
5. *Check:* $45 × 40 = $1,800

The holiday party cost $45 for each employee.

Solve these problems using the rules stated above as a guide.

1. Five crates of parts are to be shipped by National Airways. The crates weigh 56.7 kilograms, 46.3 kilograms, 74.8 kilograms, 68.5 kilograms and 60.8 kilograms respectively.
   a. What is the total weight of the crates to be shipped?
   b. What is the average weight of the crates? Carry out the answer to 2 decimal places.

2. Daniel Durant, the maintenance plumber at the Sterling Apartments, had to replace damaged pipes in the sprinkler system. He cut and installed 5 pieces of pipe, measuring $8\frac{7}{8}$ feet, $3\frac{1}{3}$ feet, $2\frac{1}{6}$ feet, $9\frac{1}{2}$ feet, and $6\frac{2}{5}$ feet. What was the total number of feet of pipe needed to repair the sprinkler system?

3. In 1982, 12,500,000 passengers used Main Terminal Air facilities. By 1986, this number had risen to 30 million passengers for that year.
   a. What is the total increase in passenger use from 1982 to 1986?
   b. Over the four year period, what was the average annual increase in passenger use?

ANSWERS

1. a. ____________
   b. ____________
2. ____________
3. a. ____________
   b. ____________

4. The mailroom employees at King Products packed a group of catalogs in two mail bags but neglected to count the exact number shipped. Rather than unpack the bags and count the catalogs, the employees weighed the bags. If one catalog weighs $2\frac{3}{4}$ pounds and the bags weighed a total of 110 pounds, how many catalogs were shipped?

5. Maddie Loring, Paul Graham, and Hannah Barrow are business partners. Maddie is to receive one-third of the profit, Paul one-fourth of the profit, and Hannah the remainder. If the business had a profit of $110,880, how much did each partner receive?

6. Gem Industries stock closed on Friday at a price of $42\frac{5}{8}$. When trading resumed on Monday, this same stock opened at a price of $39\frac{7}{8}$. By how much was the stock down on opening?

7. A total of 5,828 people toured the plant facilities at South Service Company during their annual open house. This is 6 percent fewer people than toured during last year's open house. How many people toured last year?

8. Greta Steele, production manager at Popham Pipe Products, got an estimate of $3,500 to repair a casting machine. A rebuilt unit would cost $2\frac{1}{2}$ times as much as repairing the old machine. How much will a rebuilt casting machine cost?

9. Ernest Emporium realized a net profit of $656,000 for the year. The company bonus plan provides for one-half of the profit to be divided evenly among the eight regional managers. How much of a bonus did each manager receive?

10. Fashion-tec has a production capacity of 35,000 units a week. Their actual production last week was: Monday—3,274 units; Tuesday—2,492 units; Wednesday—3,194 units; Thursday—6,436 units; and Friday—5,432 units. (a) What was the difference between their actual production and their production capacity? (b) What was the average number of units produced a day? (Carry out your answer to the nearest tenth.)

11. Daniel & Sons has switched to a computerized accounting service. It used to take one and a half hours to produce checks for 500 employees. The computer can produce 125 checks a minute. How long will it take the computer to process the payroll checks for 500 employees?

ANSWERS

4. ______________

5. ______________

____

____

6. ______________

7. ______________

8. ______________

9. ______________

10. a. ______________

b. ______________

11. ______________

NAME DATE

SKILL BUILDER 19B

Computing Ratios and Proportions

RATIO A **ratio** is the relationship of one number to another. A ratio may be written either by separating the numbers by the word *to*, by separating the numbers by a colon (:), or by showing the relationship as a fraction.

Example: Gardner Electronics employs 30 full-time production workers, and 10 part-time production workers. What is the ratio of full-time to part-time workers?

Solution: 30 to 10 *or* 30:10 *or* $\frac{30}{10}$

If the fraction form is used to show the relationship, the fraction can be reduced, where appropriate. In this instance the ratio in fraction form can also be expressed as $\frac{3}{1}$. Only two numbers can be compared in fraction form, but when *to* or a colon is used, more than two numbers can be compared.

Example: Gardner Electronics also employs five office and clerical workers. What is the ratio of all production workers (30 + 10) to office and clerical workers?

Solution: 40 to 5 *or* 40:5

If the fraction form is used, the ratio appears as follows.

$$\frac{40}{5} \text{ which reduces to } \frac{8}{1}$$

The ratio of full-time production workers to part-time production workers to office employees appears as follows.

30 to 10 to 5 *or* 30:10:5

Example: Gardner employs 45 people in all (30 + 10 + 5). What is the ratio of each employee category (full-time production workers, part-time production workers, and office employees) to total employees?

Solution: $\frac{30 \text{ Full-time}}{45 \text{ Total}}$ $\frac{10 \text{ Part-time}}{45 \text{ Total}}$ $\frac{5 \text{ Office}}{45 \text{ Total}}$

PROPORTION A **proportion** is a comparison of two sets of numbers having the same ratio or relationship. In the example above, the ratio of office workers to total employees is 5:45. In fraction form, this ratio can be reduced to $\frac{1}{9}$. These two ratios, when compared, will form a proportion, and would be shown as follows.

$$\frac{5}{45} = \frac{1}{9}$$

This expression would read, "5 is to 45 as 1 is to 9." Since the ratio, or relationship, is the same between the two sets of numbers, their cross products will be equal. In cross multiplication, the numerator of each ratio is multiplied by the denominator of the other ratio. The resulting products must be equal for the ratios to be a true proportion.

$$\frac{5}{45} \times \frac{1}{9} \qquad 5 \times 9 = 45 \qquad 1 \times 45 = 45$$

The two ratios are in proportion.

Where two sets of numbers should be proportional, but one set is incomplete, the unknown value can be found by cross-multiplying in a proportion.

Example: Gardner Electronics is planning an increase in its production line. Three wrapping machines require an area of 28 square meters. How much space must they provide for a total of 12 wrapping machines?

Solution:

Known

Number of machines presently in use—3
Number of machines to be used—12
Area required for 3 machines—28 square meters

Unknown

Area required for 12 machines

Ratios

The ratios involved are 12 machines to 3 machines and ? square meters to 28 square meters. The proportion would be 12 is to 3 as ? is to 28.

1. $\frac{12}{3} = \frac{?}{28}$

2. Cross multiply 12 by 28: $12 \times 28 = 336$.

3. Place this product over the denominator 3, and carry out the division.

$$\frac{336}{3} = 112 \text{ square meters}$$

4. ***Check:*** $\frac{12}{3} = \frac{112}{28}$ $\qquad 12 \times 28 = 336$ $\qquad 3 \times 112 = 336$

Twelve machines would require 112 square meters of floor space.

Using ratio and proportion, solve these problems.

ANSWERS

1. ______________________
2. ______________________
3. ______________________
4. ______________________
5. ______________________
6. ______________________
7. ______________________
8. ______________________
9. ______________________
10. ______________________

1. It takes 16 production workers to produce 48 parts in one hour. How many workers would be needed to produce 144 parts in one hour?

2. A new delivery van used 25 liters of gasoline to travel 290 kilometers. How far can the van travel on 60 liters of gasoline?

3. Hamburger Heaven can prepare 136 portions from 34 pounds of ground beef. How many portions can be prepared from 110 pounds of ground beef?

4. A quality check found 21 transformers defective out of a production run of 840. Inspection of a second lot found 67 defective units. Assuming a uniform defect rate, how many transformers were in the second lot?

5. A builder's plan calls for 13 sheets of plywood to cover an area of 416 square feet. How many sheets will be required to cover 992 square feet?

6. A study has shown that a group of 50 people require $1\frac{2}{3}$ hours to tour the backstage area at the Civic Center for the Performing Arts. How many people can take this tour in an 8-hour period?

7. The wrapping machines at Gardner Electronics use 18 spools of wrapping material in $2\frac{1}{4}$ hours. How many spools of wrapping material will be needed for $7\frac{3}{4}$ hours of operation?

8. Ocean Cold Canneries has determined that 75 labels are damaged for every 5,000 cans of fish processed. If 279 labels were damaged, how many cans of fish were processed in this batch?

9. Classic Clothes used 279 meters of fabric to produce 620 pairs of slacks. How many meters of fabric will they need to produce 1,200 pairs of slacks?

10. The wholesale price of 2 shirts is $27. How many shirts are in an order costing $216?

NAME DATE

SKILL BUILDER — Checking Accounts and Bank Records — 20A

A **deposit slip** is the record of money put into a checking account. A **check** is the record of money taken out of an account. To keep track of deposits made, checks written, and the balance on hand, the depositor uses a **checkbook stub** or **check register.** The stub or register entries should always be filled out before the check is written. Whenever a deposit is made, the amount is added to the balance shown on the stub and totaled. The amount of the next check is then deducted from this new balance. Any money collected by the bank for the depositor must be added to the balance, and any charges the bank makes for its services should be deducted from the balance. It is important to properly identify each transaction and to add or subtract as the nature of the transaction requires.

1. This check register shows various checks written and deposits made. The balance before check number 576 is $485.14. Assuming all entries are correctly written, what is the balance remaining after check number 581 is written?

RECORD ALL CHARGES OR CREDITS THAT AFFECT YOUR ACCOUNT

NO.	DATE	ISSUED TO OR DESCRIPTION OF DEPOSIT	AMOUNT OF PAYMENT	✓	OTHER DEDUCT.	AMOUNT OF DEPOSIT	BALANCE FORWARD 485.14
576	6/2	To Connally-Wright For Insurance	112.75				
577	6/3	To MasterCard For May statement	116.86				
	6/5	To Deposit For —				175.00	
578	6/6	To United Campaign For Contribution	10.00				
579	6/8	To Public Gas & Electric Co. For May Electric & Gas	75.00				
	6/12	To Deposit For —				300.00	
580	6/15	To State Motor Vehicle Div. For License renewal	19.50				
581	6/18	To West-Penn Oil Co. For Fill fuel-oil tank	343.20				
		To For					
		To For					

2. The nine check stubs on page 88 are from Portland Pottery. The amount of each check and deposit has been properly recorded. The balance before check number 535 is $1,240.78. What is the balance after check number 543 is written?

NO. 535 $ 10.50
DATE January 29, 19 —
TO City Clerk
FOR Permit

	DOLLARS	CENTS
BALANCE		
AMT. DEPOSITED	695	96
TOTAL		
AMT. THIS CHECK		
BALANCE		

NO. 536 $ 69.84
DATE January 29, 19 —
TO Perry Press
FOR Advertising flyers

	DOLLARS	CENTS
BALANCE		
AMT. DEPOSITED		
TOTAL		
AMT. THIS CHECK		
BALANCE		

NO. 537 $ 33.45
DATE January 30, 19 —
TO Postal Service
FOR Postage

	DOLLARS	CENTS
BALANCE		
AMT. DEPOSITED		
TOTAL		
AMT. THIS CHECK		
BALANCE		

NO. 538 $ 580.16
DATE January 30, 19 —
TO Champion Sales
FOR Shirts-Invoice 873A

	DOLLARS	CENTS
BALANCE		
AMT. DEPOSITED	326 246	59 74
TOTAL		
AMT. THIS CHECK		
BALANCE		

NO. 539 $ 118.91
DATE February 8, 19 —
TO Headley Paper Co
FOR Wrapping supplies

	DOLLARS	CENTS
BALANCE		
AMT. DEPOSITED		
TOTAL		
AMT. THIS CHECK		
BALANCE		

NO. 540 $ 481.05
DATE February 18, 19 —
TO City Tax Collector
FOR First quarter tax

	DOLLARS	CENTS
BALANCE		
AMT. DEPOSITED		
TOTAL		
AMT. THIS CHECK		
BALANCE		

NO. 541 $ 105.21
DATE February 21, 19 —
TO National Telephone Co.
FOR January bill

	DOLLARS	CENTS
BALANCE		
AMT. DEPOSITED		
TOTAL		
AMT. THIS CHECK		
BALANCE		

NO. 542 $ 211.97
DATE February 23, 19 —
TO Eastern Power and Light Co
FOR Electric bill

	DOLLARS	CENTS
BALANCE		
AMT. DEPOSITED	659 411	28 85
TOTAL		
AMT. THIS CHECK		
BALANCE		

NO. 543 $ 429.85
DATE February 27, 19 —
TO Motors Acceptance Corp
FOR Truck payment

	DOLLARS	CENTS
BALANCE		
AMT. DEPOSITED	896	51
TOTAL		
AMT. THIS CHECK		
BALANCE		

NAME DATE

SKILL BUILDER — Bank Statement Reconciliation — 20B

Every month the bank sends a statement for each checking account, summarizing all transactions that have taken place since the previous statement. The bank statement should promptly be compared to the checkbook record. Adjusting the checkbook balance and the bank statement balance is called **reconciliation.** The differences in the balances that may appear can be due to outstanding checks written but not yet cleared by the bank, deposits in transit (deposits made too late to be included on the statement), service charges, credits, or interest earned on the account.

A typical bank statement is shown below along with the form printed on the back, which is used to assist in reconciling the account. The bank statement shows a balance of $515.67. The balance on the last checkbook entry is $528.95. Use these steps in reconciling the balances.

1. Write the bank statement balance at A on the reconciliation form.
2. Compare the bank statement and checkbook record. List any deposits not shown on the bank statement **(deposits in transit),** and total them at B. (A deposit of $250 was made late on October 10 and is not shown on the bank statement.)
3. Determine the subtotal by adding the statement balance and deposits in transit (A + B). Write the subtotal at C.
4. List any outstanding checks (three checks are outstanding, #442 for $49.42, #452 for $37.07, and #453 for $24.74 totaling $111.23), and enter the total at D.
5. Deduct the total of outstanding checks (D) from the subtotal (C).
6. Total all credits and corrections on bank statement that increase the balance in the checkbook (Automatic transfer—$126.59 and NOW interest $4.08). Add this total to the checkbook balance.
7. Total all charges and fees on the bank statement ($5.18 service charge), and subtract this amount from the checkbook balance.
8. The adjusted balances should now agree.

FIRST NATIONAL BANK OF SECAUCUS
526 Franklin Avenue
Secaucus, NJ 07094
(201) 555-1717

Reginald Perry
532 Sesame Lane
Secaucus, NJ 07094

ON	YOUR BALANCE WAS	NO.	WE SUBTRACTED CHECKS TOTALING	LESS ACTIVITY CHARGE	NO.	WE ADDED DEPOSITS OF	MAKING YOUR PRESENT BALANCE
Sep.10,19--	561.71	15	1220.77	0.00	4	1174.73	515.67

DATE	CHECKS			DEPOSITS	BALANCE
Sep. 10					561.71
Sep. 11	27.19				534.52
Sep. 16				318.53	853.05
Sep. 18	4.00	22.20			826.85
Sep. 21	15.00				811.85
Sep. 22	25.00			126.59(T)	913.44
Sep. 24	124.45	5.18(S)			783.81
Sep. 25	24.05				759.76
Sep. 30				225.00	984.76
Oct. 1	5.10	10.00	29.40	500.53	1440.79
Oct. 6	443.80				996.99
Oct. 7	18.99	100.00			878.00
Oct. 8	101.84	264.57			511.59
Oct. 10				4.08(I)	515.67

BANK RECONCILIATION FORM

Bank Statement Balance → 515.67 A

Period ended

Add deposits in transit.

Date of deposit:	Amount.
10/10	250.00
Total	250.00 B

Total (A plus B) → 765.67 C

List outstanding checks.

Check No.	Amount.
442	49.42
452	37.07
453	24.74
Total	111.23 D

Current Bank Balance (C minus D) → 654.44

Checkbook	$528.95
⑥ Credit	+ 130.67
	659.62
⑦ Service charge	− 5.18
	$654.44

Complete the following bank reconciliations.

1. Carol Naster's bank statement showed a balance of $605.50, from which a service charge of $7.50 had been deducted. Carol's checkbook showed a balance of $448.16. Three checks were outstanding, totaling $164.84.

2. Daubner Dairies' bank statement showed a balance of $1,755.97. Two notes for $300 and $515 had been collected by the bank that month, and credited to the account. There was a collection charge of $7.50 and a service charge of $4.50. The checkbook balance was $765.53. Outstanding checks totaled $187.44.

BANK RECONCILIATION FORM

Bank Statement Balance → ______ A

Period ended ______ Add deposits in transit.

Date of deposit: ______ Amount ______

Total ______ B

Total (A plus B) → ______ C

List outstanding checks.

Check No. ______ Amount ______

Total ______ D

Current Bank Balance (C minus D) → ______

BANK RECONCILIATION FORM

Bank Statement Balance → ______ A

Period ended ______ Add deposits in transit.

Date of deposit: ______ Amount ______

Total ______ B

Total (A plus B) → ______ C

List outstanding checks.

Check No. ______ Amount ______

Total ______ D

Current Bank Balance (C minus D) → ______

3. Julia Fanter's checkbook showed a balance of $224.03. The bank statement indicated a balance of $312.45, which included a service charge of $5.42. Two checks were outstanding totaling $309, and Julia's deposit of $215.16, dated April 25, was in transit.

4. The Corliss Corporation received its monthly bank statement showing a balance of $4,055.16. A $50 check which had been deposited was returned for insufficient funds. The bank also collected a $125 note for Corliss, for which they charged $3.50. The checkbook balance was $4,026.36, with outstanding checks totaling $157.30. There was a deposit in transit in the amount of $200 dated January 30.

BANK RECONCILIATION FORM

Bank Statement Balance → ______ A

Period ended ______ Add deposits in transit.

Date of deposit: ______ Amount ______

Total ______ B

Total (A plus B) → ______ C

List outstanding checks.

Check No. ______ Amount ______

Total ______ D

Current Bank Balance (C minus D) → ______

BANK RECONCILIATION FORM

Bank Statement Balance → ______ A

Period ended ______ Add deposits in transit.

Date of deposit: ______ Amount ______

Total ______ B

Total (A plus B) → ______ C

List outstanding checks.

Check No. ______ Amount ______

Total ______ D

Current Bank Balance (C minus D) → ______

NAME DATE

SKILL BUILDER

Payroll Plans

21A

HOURLY RATE PAYROLL PLAN Many employees are paid a fixed hourly rate of pay, or a **regular hourly wage rate. Total (gross) earnings** are calculated by multiplying the hours worked by the wage for each hour worked.

Example: Nannette Moreno worked the following hours one week: 8, 7, 8, 7, and 8 hours. At a rate of $6.30 an hour, how much did she earn that week?

Solution: 8 + 7 + 8 + 7 + 8 = 38 hours

$6.30	Hourly rate
×38	Hours
$239.40	Gross earnings

OVERTIME Employees receive their regular wage rate for time worked within the normal workweek, which is usually 40 hours. Time worked beyond the normal 40 hours is called **overtime.**

Federal law provides that employees shall be paid at a rate at least 50 percent greater than their regular hourly rate for all hours in excess of 40 hours. This is called **time and a half.** For example, at time and a half, a normal hourly rate of $6.40 would be an overtime rate of $9.60 an hour ($6.40 × 1.5 = $9.60). (When employees work on Sundays or holidays, they sometimes receive overtime rates that are double the regular hourly rate.)

Example: During the current week, Dee Morrison worked 45 hours. If her regular hourly rate is $5.80, what were her gross earnings for the week if she is paid time and a half for all hours worked over 40?

Solution:

Regular earnings	40 hours × $5.80 =	$232.00
Overtime rate	$5.80 × 1.5 = $8.70	
Overtime earnings	5 hours × $8.70 =	43.50
Total gross earnings		$275.50

Complete the following partial payroll registers to find each employee's **gross earnings.** The employee's actual take-home pay will be less than the gross earnings once deductions are made for social security, income taxes, and so on. The regular rate is based on a 40-hour week, with time and a half for all hours in excess of 40 hours a week.

1.

ISLER MANUFACTURING COMPANY
WEEK ENDING MAY 18, 19—

EMPLOYEE NUMBER	HOURS WORKED					REGULAR HOURS	HOURLY RATE	GROSS EARNINGS
	M	T	W	T	F			
375	8	8	8	8	8	________	$8.00	________
411	8	8	8	8	4	________	6.25	________
465	8	$7\frac{1}{2}$	8	6	8	________	6.10	________
505	4	4	8	8	8	________	8.45	________
573	8	8	7	8	8	________	6.38	________
							Total	________

2.

EMPLOYEE NUMBER	HOURS WORKED					TIME		HOURLY RATE	WAGE		GROSS EARNINGS
	M	T	W	T	F	REGULAR	OVERTIME		REGULAR	OVERTIME	
110	8	8	8	8	8	______	______	$5.95	______	______	______
111	8	8	8	9	4	______	______	5.70	______	______	______
112	8	9	9	8	8	______	______	6.20	______	______	______
113	9	10	8	9	8	______	______	5.80	______	______	______
114	3	8	9	9	10	______	______	6.90	______	______	______
115	10	9	9	9	9	______	______	6.20	______	______	______
116	8	8	8	8	8	______	______	6.75	______	______	______
117	—	10	10	9	9	______	______	6.50	______	______	______
118	8	9	$8\frac{1}{2}$	8	8	______	______	6.00	______	______	______
119	9	9	9	9	7	______	______	6.40	______	______	______
								Totals	______	______	______

PIECE-WORK PAYROLL PLAN Manufacturing employees are sometimes paid according to the number of items they complete. This is the **piece-work wage** plan. The rate paid may vary with the difficulty of the task or the experience of the employee.

Example: During a 5-day workweek, Marv Grasso completed 74 items. During the same week, Betty Woodson completed 99 of the same items. If the rate for each piece was $2.775, what were the gross earnings of these workers?

Solution:
74 × $2.775 = $205.35 for Grasso
99 × $2.775 = $274.725 → $274.73 for Woodson

3. A partial payroll register is shown below. Determine the total number of articles made by each employee. Determine gross earnings by multiplying total articles times rate. Round off gross earnings to the nearest cent.

SINGLETON INSTRUMENT COMPANY
PAYROLL REGISTER

EMPLOYEE NUMBER	NUMBER OF ARTICLES					TOTAL ARTICLES	RATE	GROSS EARNINGS
	M	T	W	T	F			
51	24	22	25	21	25	______	$2.00	______
52	24	25	20	23	—	______	2.20	______
53	28	25	26	25	22	______	2.10	______
54	19	22	20	24	26	______	2.25	______
55	22	25	23	19	16	______	2.455	______
56	23	—	20	17	25	______	2.50	______
57	24	28	29	24	25	______	2.25	______
58	25	21	26	26	24	______	2.775	______
							Total	______

NAME DATE

SKILL BUILDER 21B

Payroll Deductions

PAYROLL REGISTER A payroll register is shown on page 94. Notice that there are four columns in the Employee Data section. The No. column is for recording the number assigned to each employee by the employer. The next column contains the employee's name. The Marital Status column shows whether the employee is married or single. The Exemp. column indicates the number of tax exemptions (self, spouse, children) claimed by the employee.

The Earnings section contains three columns. The Regular column shows the employee's regular earnings—hours worked times hourly wage. The Overtime column shows any overtime earned. The Total column shows the employee's total earnings—regular wages plus overtime. If there is no overtime, the figure in the Total column will be the same as the figure in the Regular column.

The Deductions section contains six columns. The Income Tax column shows the amount of federal income tax deducted from the employee's total earnings. The amount to be deducted can be found by using the tables found below. Notice that separate tables are used for taxpayers claiming single and married marital status. Notice, too, that there are columns for the number of exemptions claimed by the employee. FICA tax (social security) is deducted from the employee's total earnings to provide a fund for retired and disabled workers. The amount of the FICA deduction is 7.51 percent (0.0751) of the employee's total earnings. The amount of FICA tax to be deducted can be found by using the table on page 65. All amounts are rounded off to the nearest cent.

MBA (Mutual Benefit Association) is a voluntary program whereby employees contribute 1 percent of their regular earnings to a fund to provide compensation for work-related injuries. The Union Dues column records the amount deducted from union members' earnings on the last paycheck of the month. Union members pay $10 a month for union dues.

State tax is the amount of state income tax withheld from the employee's total earnings. The total of all deductions—income tax, FICA tax, MBA, union dues, and state tax—is recorded in the Total column.

The Amount column in the Net Pay section shows the employee's actual take-home pay. It records total earnings minus total deductions. The number of the employee's paycheck is recorded in the Ck. No. column.

SINGLE Persons–**WEEKLY** Payroll Period

(For Wages Paid After December 1987)

And the wages are–		And the number of withholding allowances claimed is–										
At least	But less than	0	1	2	3	4	5	6	7	8	9	10
		The amount of income tax to be withheld shall be–										
240	250	34	28	22	17	11	6	0	0	0	0	0
250	260	35	30	24	18	13	7	1	0	0	0	0
260	270	37	31	25	20	14	9	3	0	0	0	0
270	280	38	33	27	21	16	10	4	0	0	0	0
280	290	40	34	28	23	17	12	6	0	0	0	0
290	300	41	36	30	24	19	13	7	2	0	0	0
300	310	43	37	31	26	20	15	9	3	0	0	0
310	320	44	39	33	27	22	16	10	5	0	0	0
320	330	46	40	34	29	23	18	12	6	1	0	0
330	340	47	42	36	30	25	19	13	8	2	0	0

MARRIED Persons–**WEEKLY** Payroll Period

(For Wages Paid After December 1987)

And the wages are–		And the number of withholding allowances claimed is–										
At least	But less than	0	1	2	3	4	5	6	7	8	9	10
		The amount of income tax to be withheld shall be–										
230	240	26	21	15	10	4	0	0	0	0	0	0
240	250	28	22	17	11	5	0	0	0	0	0	0
250	260	29	24	18	13	7	1	0	0	0	0	0
260	270	31	25	20	14	8	3	0	0	0	0	0
270	280	32	27	21	16	10	4	0	0	0	0	0
280	290	34	28	23	17	11	6	0	0	0	0	0
290	300	35	30	24	19	13	7	2	0	0	0	0
300	310	37	31	26	20	14	9	3	0	0	0	0
310	320	38	33	27	22	16	10	5	0	0	0	0
320	330	40	34	29	23	17	12	6	1	0	0	0
330	340	41	36	30	25	19	13	8	2	0	0	0

1. Complete the payroll register below. Determine total earnings, amounts of deductions, total deductions, and the amount of net pay. The state income tax is 1.1 percent of total earnings. Check numbers will begin with 1411. Total all money columns.

PAYROLL REGISTER

For the Week Beginning June 17, 19 — and Ending June 23, 19 — Paid June 28, 19 —

EMPLOYEE DATA					EARNINGS			DEDUCTIONS						NET PAY	
NO.	NAME	MARITAL STATUS	EXEMP.	HOURS	REGULAR	OVERTIME	TOTAL	INCOME TAX	FICA TAX	MBA	UNION DUES	STATE TAX	TOTAL	AMOUNT	CK. NO.
111	Ahrend, M.	M	2	40	286.00	—.00				2.86	10.00				
112	Blase, G.	M	3	40	300.00	—.00				3.00	—.00				
117	Charlton, H.	S	0	42	272.00	20.40				—.00	10.00				
120	Dulong, R.	M	4	41	284.00	10.65				2.84	10.00				
121	Frisch, V.	S	3	42	264.00	19.80				2.64	10.00				
124	Garth, M.	M	2	38	281.20	—.00				—.00	10.00				
130	Lennis, J.	M	4	44	248.00	37.20				2.48	10.00				
132	Mild, S.	S	0	40	296.00	—.00				—.00	—.00				
135	Milton, F.	M	3	41	274.00	10.28				2.74	10.00				
136	Pilcher, D.	S	2	37	279.35	—.00				2.79	10.00				
142	Popham, P.	S	1	40	282.00	—.00				2.82	10.00				
148	Quentin, F.	M	5	43	256.00	28.80				2.56	10.00				
149	Ridley, J.	M	1	40	280.00	—.00				2.80	—.00				
152	Scott, W.	M	3	42	260.00	19.50				—.00	—.00				
154	Willard, J.	S	2	44	250.00	37.50				2.50	10.00				
	Totals														

NAME DATE

SKILL BUILDER 22A

Taking Inventory

STOCK CARDS Every business must know how much merchandise, or stock, it has on hand at a given time. Computerized cash registers have made the task of maintaining a running inventory of stock much easier today. Data is entered into the computerized cash register, and it is reported on **stock cards,** which are a record of the inventory on hand. Because the data is subject to error when a person enters it into the machine, it must be verified.

Each stock card indicates a minimum stock amount. When stock for a particular item falls below the minimum amount, that item must be reordered.

For the four stock cards shown, verify the balance on each date, and make any corrections by crossing out the incorrect balance and writing the correct balance next to it. Circle the date on which any item falls below the minimum.

1.

Merchandise *Air Conditioner*

Minimum *36*

Date	Quantity Received	Quantity Sold	Balance
19– 3/2			30
3/4	15		45
3/8	18	10	53
3/15	25	36	64
3/19	20	28	56
3/26	12		68
3/29	36	24	70

2.

Merchandise *Bicycle*

Minimum *140*

Date	Quantity Received	Quantity Sold	Balance
19– 3/3			155
3/9		110	265
3/16	120		145
3/18	120	90	175
3/21		40	135
3/25	180	50	265
3/30		75	190

3.

Merchandise *Clock*

Minimum *72*

Date	Quantity Received	Quantity Sold	Balance
19– 3/1			81
3/5		36	45
3/9	40		85
3/13	114	72	117
3/22		50	67
3/27	50	40	77

4.

Merchandise *Soccer Ball*

Minimum *70*

Date	Quantity Received	Quantity Sold	Balance
19– 3/1			98
3/2	26		124
3/11		48	76
3/23	30	45	61
3/24	59		120
3/28		40	160

PHYSICAL INVENTORY No matter what system is used for maintaining a running inventory, there are bound to be errors due to theft, breakage, mistakes in recording, and so on. To correct these errors, an actual count, or **physical inventory,** must be made of goods on hand. This is usually done at specified intervals but must be done whenever an accurate financial statement must be prepared.

The two pages shown are part of the physical inventory taken at the end of the year. Check all extensions for accuracy, and enter any corrections in the space provided.

5.

PHYSICAL INVENTORY COUNT

SECTION Dinnerware PART 12
DATE Dec. 31, 19— SHEET NO. 3

COUNTED BY: F.H. RECORDED BY: E.J. COMPUTED BY: M.A.

STOCK NO.	QUANTITY	DESCRIPTION	UNIT PRICE	VALUE	CORRECTED VALUE
24	20 sets	Lily	$ 27.88	$ 557.60	______
33	23 sets	Stafford	62.00	1,326.00	______
61	17 sets	Ironstone	89.00	1,513.00	______
64	9 sets	Stoneware	54.40	504.27	______
72	13 sets	Fuji	39.79	572.27	______
80	39 sets	Pagoda	79.78	3,111.42	______
93	11 sets	Bavaria	113.75	1,221.55	______
		Total		$10,105.67	______

6.

PHYSICAL INVENTORY COUNT

SECTION Floor coverings PART 15
DATE Dec. 31, 19— SHEET NO. 5

COUNTED BY: M.R. RECORDED BY: R.G. COMPUTED BY: M.M.

STOCK NO.	QUANTITY	DESCRIPTION	AREA OF EACH	UNIT PRICE	VALUE OF EACH UNIT	TOTAL VALUE	CORRECTED TOTAL VALUE
103	12	Carstar vinyl	99 sq ft	$ 0.43 a sq ft	$ 42.57	$ 510.84	______
113	16	Bandon vinyl	99 sq ft	0.27 a sq ft	26.73	427.68	______
124	15	Econo vinyl	126 sq ft	2.17 a sq yd	30.38	4,231.50	______
162	9	Runners	42 sq ft	0.38 a sq ft	15.96	146.44	______
171	20	Manor tile, 12 × 12 in.	45 sq ft	0.39 a sq ft	17.55	351.00	______
178	19	Guild tile, 12 × 12 in.	25 sq ft	1.25 a sq ft	31.25	593.75	______
202	7	Drew tile, 12 × 12 in.	25 sq ft	0.95 a sq ft	23.75	166.25	______
204	43	Nylon shag	12 sq yd	16.49 a sq yd	197.88	8,508.84	______
255	27	Nylon broadloom	180 sq ft	17.93 a sq yd	358.60	9,682.20	______
		Total				$24,618.50	______

NAME DATE

SKILL BUILDER 22B

Valuing Inventory

COST PRICE METHOD The **cost price** is the price the retailer pays for an item. To find the inventory value, multiply the unit cost of each item by the number of items on hand. To find the total inventory value, add the inventory values of all items.

QUANTITY PURCHASED	ITEM	UNIT COST	ON HAND	INVENTORY VALUE
27 cases	Spinach	$ 7.54 a case	11 cases	$ 82.94
36 cases	Beans	7.00 a case	21 cases	147.00
21 cases	Tuna	28.90 a case	9 cases	260.10
6 cases	Clams	17.80 a case	4 cases	71.20
			Total	$561.24

Compute the inventory value of each item, and find the total inventory value for the following inventory sheets.

1.

INVENTORY REPORT AS OF JULY 1, 19—

SECTION: Music BIN NO.: 665

PURCHASE ORDER NO.	QUANTITY PURCHASED	ITEM	UNIT COST	ON HAND	INVENTORY VALUE
316	48	Carrying Cases	$17.50	12	________
316	72	Albums	8.18	39	________
358	24	Cassette Tapes	9.13	9	________
358	36	Needles	18.11	15	________
473	15 doz	Cleaning Cloths	12.00/doz	$4\frac{1}{2}$ doz	________
				Total	________

2.

INVENTORY REPORT AS OF JULY 1, 19—

SECTION: Sporting Goods BIN NO.: 758

PURCHASE ORDER NO.	QUANTITY PURCHASED	ITEM	UNIT COST	ON HAND	INVENTORY VALUE
516	8 doz	Tennis Balls	$ 36.00/doz	$3\frac{1}{2}$ doz	________
516	9 doz	Baseballs	14.40/doz	$4\frac{3}{4}$ doz	________
517	10 doz	Softballs	44.50/doz	5 doz	________
534	5 doz	Aluminum Bats	174.00/doz	$\frac{1}{2}$ doz	________
534	7 doz	Running Socks	27.00/doz	$2\frac{1}{4}$ doz	________
				Total	________

AVERAGE INVENTORY METHOD Merchandise purchased at different times may not have the same cost. When it is impractical to keep track of each purchase and its sale, the average inventory value method can be used.

Example: What is the value of the inventory of paint brushes as of June 30?

ITEM Paint brush		LOCATION BIN NO. 772		MAX. 1200 MIN. 300	
DATE	QUANTITY IN	UNIT COST	REQ. NO.	QUANTITY OUT	BALANCE
19—					
5/15	350	$1.75			350
5/28			12	113	237
6/3	450	1.80			687
6/10	450	1.90			1,137
6/15			15	975	162
6/30	300	2.00			462

Solution: First find the value of all units purchased at each price. Total the number of units and the inventory values.

No. of Units	×	***Unit Cost***	=	***Inventory Value***
350	×	$1.75	=	$ 612.50
450	×	1.80	=	810.00
450	×	1.90	=	855.00
300	×	2.00	=	600.00
1,550			=	$2,877.50

Then divide the total inventory value by the total number of units to find the average unit cost of each unit. Round to three decimal places.

Total Inventory Value	÷	***Total Units***	=	***Average Unit Cost***
$2,877.50	÷	1,550	=	$1.8564516 → $1.856

To find the inventory value on June 30, multiply the number of units on hand by the average unit cost.

Units on Hand	×	***Average Unit Cost***	=	***Inventory Value***
462	×	$1.856	=	$857.472 → $857.47

Compute the average inventory value for each of the following inventories. Round off the average unit cost to 3 decimal places, where necessary.

ANSWERS

3. ____________

4. ____________

3.

ITEM Fertilizer				
DATE	QUANTITY IN	UNIT COST	QUANTITY OUT	BALANCE
19—				
3/30	360 bags	$ 7.20		360
4/5			315	45
4/13	300 bags	8.80		345
4/18			295	50
4/27	530 bags	8.00		580
5/5			400	180
5/25	160 bags	10.30		340
5/29			100	240
6/8	400 bags	9.20		640
6/17			250	390
7/6	250 bags	8.40		640
7/30			150	490

4.

ITEM Bicycle pump				
DATE	QUANTITY IN	UNIT COST	QUANTITY OUT	BALANCE
19—				
4/1	43	$6.19		43
4/7	154	6.19		________
4/16			26	________
4/23			41	________
4/28	180	6.27		________
5/5	40	6.25		________
5/21			112	________
5/30	100	7.11	56	________

NAME DATE

SKILL BUILDER — Computing Markup — 23A

MARKUP BASED ON COST PRICE Retailers make a profit and cover their expenses by charging more for a product than they pay for it. The amount added to the cost price is the **markup.** The markup rate is called the **percent of markup,** which can be based on the cost price or on the selling price.

Example: An item costs $37.50; its selling price is $43.75. Find (a) the markup and (b) the rate of markup based on the cost price.

Solution:		
	Selling price	$43.75
	Cost price	−37.50
	Markup	$6.25

Rate of Markup Based on Cost Price	=	*Markup*	÷	*Cost Price*
?	=	$6.25	÷	$37.50
?	=	$16\frac{2}{3}$% or 16.67%		

Most retail merchants use the rate of markup based on cost to determine their selling price. For example, if a retail merchant decides that all items must have a 25 percent markup based on cost, an item costing $24 would be sold for $30.

$24 × 0.25 = $6 $24 + $6 = $30

If the same merchant decides to use a 50 percent markup based on cost, the item costing $24 would sell for $36.

$24 × 0.50 = $12 $24 + $12 = $36

1. Julie Carter purchased radios for $18 each and sold them for $24.
a. Find the markup.
b. Find the rate of markup to the nearest hundredth of a percent based on cost price.

2. Pierre Products purchased electric typewriters for $150 each and sold them for $191.60.
a. Find the markup.
b. Find the rate of markup to the nearest hundredth of a percent based on cost price.

3. Caryl Clothes purchased a dozen blouses at $216 a dozen. Each blouse retailed for $23.31. What was the rate of markup to the nearest tenth of a percent based on cost price?

4. Goliath Corp., purchased a gross of calculators for $3,730. (There are 144 items in a gross.) The calculators will be priced at a markup of $37\frac{1}{2}$ percent of the cost price. What will be the selling price of each calculator?

5. The Alberta Shoe Emporium realizes a profit of $13 on each pair of a certain style of shoe that it sells. This represents a 50 percent markup based on the cost price.
a. What is the cost price of each pair of shoes?
b. What is the selling price of each pair?

ANSWERS

1. a. ____________
   b. ____________
2. a. ____________
   b. ____________
3. ____________
4. ____________
5. a. ____________
   b. ____________

MARKUP BASED ON SELLING PRICE Markup can also be based on the selling price, or retail price, of the goods.

Example: Find the rate of markup based on the selling price for a bicycle that cost \$75 and that sells for \$87.50.

Solution:

Selling price	\$87.50
Cost price	−75.00
Markup	\$12.50

Rate of Markup Based on Selling Price	=	*Markup*	÷	*Selling Price*
?	=	\$12.50	÷	\$87.50
?	=	14.29%		

6. Portable typewriters cost a dealer \$144 each. The markup is \$66.
   a. What is the selling price of each typewriter?
   b. What is the rate of markup to the nearest hundredth of a percent based on the selling price?

7. A living room chair cost \$270 and sells for \$324.
   a. What is the amount of the markup?
   b. What is the rate of markup to the nearest hundredth of a percent based on the selling price?

ANSWERS

6. a. __________
   b. __________
7. a. __________
   b. __________

FINDING MARKUP AND SELLING PRICE

Cost Price divided by Cost Price (expressed as a percent of Selling Price) will give the amount of Selling Price.

Example: A radio cost \$37.50 and will be sold at a markup of 25 percent based on the selling price. Find the markup and the selling price.

Solution:

Selling price	100%	
Markup	−25%	of selling price
Cost price	75%	of selling price

Selling Price	=	*Cost Price*	÷	*Percent Cost Price is of Selling Price*
?	=	\$37.50	÷	75%
?	=	\$50.00		

\$50.00	Selling price
−37.50	Cost price
\$12.50	Markup

8. A suitcase cost \$43.56 and was sold at a markup of 50 percent of the selling price.
   a. What was the selling price?
   b. What was the amount of markup?

9. A digital alarm clock cost \$18 and was sold at a markup of 40 percent of the selling price.
   a. What was the selling price?
   b. What was the amount of markup?

10. Complete this table. Round off the rate to the nearest hundredth of a percent, where necessary.

ANSWERS

8. a. __________
   b. __________
9. a. __________
   b. __________

	COST PRICE	MARKUP	SELLING PRICE	RATE OF MARKUP BASED ON COST PRICE	RATE OF MARKUP BASED ON SELLING PRICE
a.	\$ 86.40	______	\$ 103.68	______	______
b.	46.20	6.60	______	______	______
c.	______	2.48	______	16%	______
d.	______	4.80	______	______	$8\frac{3}{4}$%

NAME DATE

SKILL BUILDER — Computing Markdown — 23B

MARKDOWN To move slow-selling merchandise, a retail store can mark down the price of these items. This reduction in selling price is called **markdown**. The reduced selling price is sometimes called the **new selling price**.

Markdown is expressed either as an amount or as a rate (percent). The rate of markdown may be based on either the original selling price, or on the new or reduced selling price. The dollar differences are the same, but using the reduced selling price gives the impression of a larger markdown.

Example: An item that sells for $10 is marked down to $8. What is the markdown and the rate of markdown based on the new selling price?

Solution:

Original selling price	$10
New selling price	−8
Markdown	$ 2

$$\text{Rate of Markdown} = \frac{\text{Markdown}}{\text{New Selling Price}}$$

$$? = \frac{\$2}{\$8}$$

$$? = 0.25 = 25\%$$

1. Find the markdown for the merchandise below. Find the rate of markdown to the nearest tenth of a percent, on both original selling price and new selling price.

	ORIGINAL SELLING PRICE	NEW SELLING PRICE	MARKDOWN	RATE OF MARKDOWN ORIGINAL PRICE	RATE OF MARKDOWN NEW PRICE
a.	$ 25.00	$ 20.00	________	________	________
b.	84.00	70.00	________	________	________
c.	99.00	88.00	________	________	________
d.	527.00	395.25	________	________	________

2. The Varsity Shop marked down golf clubs from $94.80 to $79. What was the rate of markdown based on the new selling price?

3. Billy Bootery marked down shoes from $50 to $40.
a. What was the rate of markdown based on the new selling price?
b. If the shoes were marked down an additional $15, what was the total rate of markdown based on the new selling price?
c. What was the total rate of markdown based on the original selling price?

4. A bicycle is marked down $30, which is 20 percent of the original selling price.
a. What was the original selling price?
b. What is the new selling price?

ANSWERS

2. ________
3. a. ________
   b. ________
   c. ________
4. a. ________
   b. ________

Goods are sometimes sold at a loss. When this is done, the new selling price is less than the cost of the goods. When the percent of loss is based on the new selling price, the cost price of the item is always equal to 100 percent plus the percent of loss based on the new selling price.

Example: Find the cost price of an item which was sold for $3.60 at a loss of $16\frac{2}{3}$ percent based on the selling price.

Solution:

Selling price	100%
Loss	$+16\frac{2}{3}\%$
Cost price	$116\frac{2}{3}\%$ or 116.67%

Cost Price = *New Selling Price* × *Percent Cost Price is of Selling Price*

? = \$3.60 × $116\frac{2}{3}\%$
? = \$3.60 × 1.1667
? = \$4.200 or \$4.20

Example: Find the new selling price of an item that cost \$24.64 if it is sold at a loss of $33\frac{1}{3}$ percent based on the new selling price.

Solution:

Selling price	100%
Loss	$+33\frac{1}{3}\%$
Cost price	$133\frac{1}{3}\%$ or $\frac{4}{3}$

New Selling Price = *Cost Price* ÷ *Percent Cost Price is of Selling Price*

? = \$24.64 ÷ $133\frac{1}{3}\%$
? = \$24.64 ÷ $\frac{4}{3}$
? = \$18.48

Example: Find the new selling price of an item on which the loss is \$12.32, which is $33\frac{1}{3}\%$ of the new selling price.

Solution:

New Selling Price = *Amount of Loss* ÷ *Loss as a Percent of New Selling Price*

? = \$12.32 ÷ $33\frac{1}{3}\%$
? = \$36.96

Cost = *New Selling Price* + *Amount of Loss*

? = \$36.96 + \$12.32
? = \$49.28

5. Complete the following table. Round off the rate of loss to the nearest tenth of a percent, where necessary.

	COST PRICE	NEW SELLING PRICE	LOSS	RATE OF LOSS BASED ON: COST PRICE	RATE OF LOSS BASED ON: NEW SELLING PRICE
a.	\$106.80	\$83.20	_____	_____	_____
b.	2.10	_____	0.42	_____	_____
c.	6.50	_____	_____	_____	20%
d.	_____	13.65	_____	_____	$12\frac{1}{2}\%$
e.	11.20	_____	_____	20%	_____

6. A sewing machine was sold for \$72 less than its cost price, which was $37\frac{1}{2}$ percent of the new selling price.
a. What is the new selling price?
b. What did the sewing machine cost?

7. A discontinued model typewriter was sold for \$45 less than its cost price. The loss on the sale was 25% of the cost price.
a. Find the cost.
b. Find the new selling cost.

ANSWERS

6. a. ________
b. ________
7. a. ________
b. ________

NAME DATE

SKILL BUILDER 24A

Computing Depreciation by Straight-Line and Double Declining-Balance Methods

Depreciation is the loss incurred through the decline in value of property such as machinery, equipment, and buildings. It may also be due to obsolescence, which is the outdating of something because a new development or more modern item has replaced it. Four methods of computing depreciation are the straight-line method, the double declining-balance method, the units-of-production method, and the sum-of-the-years' digits method.

STRAIGHT-LINE METHOD The **straight-line** method for computing depreciation includes the following steps.

1. Determine the probable, or **estimated life** of the property.

2. Determine the **trade-in** or **scrap value** of the item. This is an estimate of the item's worth at the end of its useful life.

3. Find the difference between the original cost and the trade-in value; divide the difference by the estimated (probable) life to find the **annual depreciation.**

4. Divide the annual depreciation by the original cost to find the **annual rate of depreciation.**

Example: A machine that cost $10,500 has a trade-in value of $1,575 at the end of 5 years. Find the annual depreciation and the rate of depreciation.

Solution:

$10,500	Original cost
−1,575	Trade-in value
$ 8,925	Depreciation for the 5-year period
$ 8,925	÷ 5 = $1,785 Annual depreciation

Rate of Depreciation	=	*Annual Depreciation*	÷	*Original Cost*
?	=	$1,785	÷	$10,500
?	=	0.17 or 17%		

ANSWERS

1. a. ____ b. ____ c. ____
2. ____

1. A station wagon costs $15,800. After 4 years it has a resale value of 30 percent of the original cost.

a. Find the resale value.

b. Find the annual depreciation.

c. Find the rate of depreciation, carried out to 1 decimal place.

2. The annual rate of depreciation on a warehouse was estimated to be 6.7 percent of the original cost. If the warehouse cost $850,000, what was the annual depreciation?

3. Complete the following straight-line depreciation schedule. Round off the rate of depreciation to the nearest tenth of a percent where necessary.

PROPERTY	ORIGINAL COST	TRADE-IN VALUE	ESTIMATED LIFE	ANNUAL DEPRECIATION	RATE OF DEPRECIATION
Truck	$ 19,600	$ 1,960	5 years	____	____
Building	$1,490,000	____	15 years	____	6.3%
Equipment	$ 198,400	38,884	____	$13,293	____

DOUBLE DECLINING-BALANCE METHOD The double declining-balance method is used to compute the annual depreciation on the decreasing value of an item. The trade-in value is not deducted from the cost of the item. This method includes the following steps.

1. Divide 100 percent by the estimated life of the item to determine the straight-line annual rate of depreciation. For example, a 5-year useful life is equal to 20 percent a year. (100% ÷ 5 = 20%)

2. Double this rate. (2 × 20% = 40%)

3. Multiply the original cost of the item by the double rate to find the first year's depreciation.

4. Subtract the first year's depreciation from the original cost to determine the value remaining at that time, which is the **book value** for the first year.

5. Repeat steps 3 and 4 for each successive year, beginning with the book value at the end of the first year. Continue this procedure until the book value equals the trade-in value.

Example: A computer that costs $3,200 is expected to last 8 years. Use the double declining-balance method to find the book value at the end of 3 years.

Solution:

1. 100% ÷ 8 = 12.5%

2. 12.5% × 2 = 25% or 0.25

3. *1st Year Depreciation* = *Cost* × *Double Rate*

? = $3,200 × 0.25

? = $ 800

4. $3,200 Cost

−800 First year depreciation

$2,400 Book value at end of first year

5. $2,400 × 0.25 = $600 Second year depreciation

$2,400 − $600 = $1,800 Book value at end of second year

$1,800 × 0.25 = $450 Third year depreciation

$1,800 − $450 = $1,350 Book value at end of third year

4. A lift truck originally cost $81,500 and has an estimated trade-in value of $7,500 after 10 years. Using the double declining-balance method, find the book value of the truck at the end of the third year.

5. Gittle Printers purchased a press for $550,000. The straight-line depreciation rate is 8 percent. Using the double declining-balance method, determine the book value at the end of the second year.

6. A cash register costing $2,500 has a trade-in value of $450 at the end of 5 years. What is its book value at the end of the fourth year if the double declining-balance method is used?

7. A computer that originally cost $13,500 is estimated to have a trade-in value of $2,500 at the end of 6 years. Using the double declining-balance method, determine its book value at the end of the fifth year. Round off percents to nearest hundredth of a percent.

ANSWERS

4. ____________

5. ____________

6. ____________

7. ____________

NAME DATE

SKILL BUILDER 24B

Computing Depreciation by Units of Production and Sum-of-the-Years' Digits Methods

UNITS OF PRODUCTION METHOD The useful life of equipment is sometimes estimated in terms of the total amount of work performed either in the number of units produced or the number of hours of operation. This way of computing depreciation is known as the **units of production** method.

If a machine wears out after it has produced 50,000 units, its **production life** would be 50,000 units. If the machine cost $28,600 and has an estimated trade-in value of $1,400, the depreciation for a year in which it produces 4,750 units is determined as follows.

$28,600	Cost
− 1,400	Trade-in value
$27,200	Total depreciation

Unit Depreciation	=	*Total Depreciation*	÷	*Production Life in Units*
?	=	$27,200	÷	50,000
?	=	$0.544		

Depreciation For Year	=	*Units Produced*	×	*Unit Depreciation Rate*
?	=	4,750	×	$0.544
?	=	$2,584		

Depreciation can also be based on hours of operation. Assume that the machine described at the left has a useful production life of 17,500 hours and that it was operated for 825 hours last year.

Hourly Depreciation	=	*Total Depreciation*	÷	*Production Life in Hours*
?	=	$27,200	÷	17,500
?	=	$1.554285 →		$1.55429

Depreciation For Year	=	*Hours Used*	×	*Hourly Depreciation*
?	=	825	×	$1.55429
?	=	$1,282.289 →		$1,282.29

1. The production life of a machine is estimated at 180,000 units. The machine costs $78,000 and has an estimated trade-in value of $6,000. Complete the depreciation schedule at the right.

YEAR	PRODUCTION	DEPRECIATION
1	5,088 units	________
2	3,510 units	________
3	4,440 units	________

2. Compute the depreciation for the same machine if its estimated production life is 42,000 hours. It was used for the periods listed at the right. Round off the hourly depreciation to 5 decimal places.

YEAR	HOURS OF USE	DEPRECIATION
1	600	________
2	2,220	________
3	1,500	________

3. A machine that cost $17,700 has an estimated production life of 25,000 hours, with no trade-in value at the end of that time. If the machine was used 680 hours last year, find the depreciation for that year. Carry out the hourly depreciation to 3 decimal places.

ANSWER

3. ________

4. An automatic casting machine has a production life of 3,000,000 units. The machine cost $75,000 and has an estimated trade-in value of $1,500. Find the depreciation if 480,000 units were produced the first year. Carry out the unit depreciation rate to 4 decimal places.

ANSWER

4. ________

THE SUM-OF-THE-YEARS' DIGITS METHOD The **sum-of-the-years' digits** method assumes the greatest depreciation for the years when an article is newest and its value is likely to drop the most. The rate of depreciation decreases each year. To compute depreciation using this method, follow these steps.

1. Estimate the useful life of the article in years.

2. Find the sum of all the digits of the years of estimated useful life. For example, for a machine with an estimated useful life of 4 years, the sum of the digits would be 1 + 2 + 3 + 4 = 10.*

3. Form a depreciation fraction by using the sum of the digits (in this case, 10) as the denominator of the fraction. The numerator is the digit of each of the individual years in reverse order: year 1 = $\frac{4}{10}$, year 2 = $\frac{3}{10}$, year 3 = $\frac{2}{10}$, and year 4 = $\frac{1}{10}$.

*$\left(\text{Sum of Digits} = \frac{N(N+1)}{2} = \frac{4(4+1)}{2} = \frac{20}{2} = 10\right)$

4. Subtract the estimated trade-in value from the original cost to find the total depreciation.

5. Multiply the total depreciation by the depreciation fraction to determine the depreciation for the first year.

6. Subtract the depreciation from the original cost to obtain the book value at the end of the first year.

7. Repeat steps 5 and 6, as necessary, to find the depreciation and book value for the required years.

Example: A truck costs $34,800. After 5 years, it will have a trade-in value of $5,900. Construct a depreciation schedule using the sum-of-the-years' digits method.

Solution: 1 + 2 + 3 + 4 + 5 = 15

$34,800	Cost
−5,900	Trade-in value
$28,900	Total depreciation

YEAR	DEPRECIATION	BOOK VALUE AT END OF YEAR
1	5/15 × $28,900 = $9,633.33	$34,800.00 − $9,633.33 = $25,166.67
2	4/15 × 28,900 = 7,706.67	25,166.67 − 7,706.67 = 17,460.00
3	3/15 × 28,900 = 5,780.00	17,460.00 − 5,780.00 = 11,680.00
4	2/15 × 28,900 = 3,853.33	11,680.00 − 3,853.33 = 7,826.67
5	1/15 × 28,900 = 1,926.67	7,826.67 − 1,926.67 = 5,900.00*

*Trade-in Value

Use the sum-of-the-years' digits method to compute depreciation in these problems.

ANSWERS

5. a. ________
   b. ________
6. a. ________
   b. ________
   c. ________

5. An item that cost $1,250 has a trade-in value of $25 at the end of 7 years.
a. Find the book value for the third year.
b. Find the amount of depreciation for the sixth year.

6. A solar heating installation cost $30,500 and has an estimated life of 20 years with a trade-in value of $2,500 at the end of that time. Find the depreciation for (a) the first year, (b) the second year, and (c) the third year.

NAME DATE

SKILL BUILDER 25A

Computing Simple Interest by Formula

Interest can be considered the rent paid to borrow money. The **principal** is the amount of money borrowed, and the **rate** is the percent of interest charged.

Time is the period of time for which the money is on loan. Since many loans are for less than one year, time may be expressed as a fraction of a year in terms of days, weeks, or months. Use this formula to compute interest.

$$\textit{Interest} = \textit{Principal} \times \textit{Rate} \times \textit{Time}$$

or

$$I = P \times R \times T$$

Example: Find the interest on $1,269 at 13 percent for 5 months.

Solution:

$$I = P \times R \times T$$

$$? = \$1{,}269 \times 0.13 \times \frac{5}{12}$$

$$? = \$68.74$$

BANKER'S YEAR When the time of the loan is expressed in days, the number of days of the loan is divided by the number of days in a year. For purposes of computing interest, a **banker's year** or **commercial year** of 360 days is used.

Example: Find the interest on $3,200 at 11 percent for 90 days, using the banker's year.

Solution:

$$I = P \times R \times T$$

$$? = \$3{,}200 \times 0.11 \times \frac{90}{360}$$

$$? = \$88$$

FINDING THE EXACT TIME The exact time is found by counting the actual number of days between any two dates, excluding the first date but including the last date.

When counting days, remember that the month of February has 29 days instead of 28 during a leap year. A leap year occurs every four years. If the number of a year is evenly divisible by 4, it is a leap year. (There is an exception. If the year ends in at least two zeros, for example, 1800, 1900, or 2000, it must be divisible by 400 to be a leap year.)

$1988 \div 4 = 497$ 1988 is a leap year

Example: Find the exact number of days between December 12, 1987, and March 28, 1988.

Solution:

From December 12	19	days left in December
	31	days in January
	29	days in February (leap year)
To March 28	28	days in March
	107	days, exact time

Compute the interest in these problems using the formula $I = P \times R \times T$. Use the banker's year (360 days) when days are indicated. Carry out percents to the nearest tenth of a percent, where necessary.

1. $1,850 at 9% for 90 days ____________

2. $600 at 11% for 75 days ____________

3. $3,500 at $13\frac{1}{2}$% for 145 days ____________

4. $7,500 at 12% for 5 months ____________

Find the exact number of days between the following dates.

5. May 5 to September 17 **6.** October 23 to January 8 **7.** July 7 to November 29

ANSWERS

5. ____________

6. ____________

7. ____________

Compute the interest due on the following loans using the bankers year and exact time.

ANSWERS

8. ____________

9. ____________

10. ____________

8. $2,400 at 10% from January 12, 19—, to May 27, 19—

9. $600 at 12.5% from August 14 to December 1

10. $11,750 at 13% from April 3 to May 27

ORDINARY INTEREST **Ordinary interest** is frequently used in business because it is easier to count the time and determine the due date of loans. Ordinary interest assumes that a year consists of 12 months of 30 days each. To find the date on which a loan is due, count forward the number of months of the loan. The loan will be due on the same day of the month as the loan began.

Example: Find the due date of a 3-month loan made on April 15.

Solution:

April 15 to May 15	1 month
May 15 to June 15	1 month
June 15 to July 15	1 month
	3 months

The loan is due on July 15.

If the month the loan is due does not contain the same last day number as the month when the loan was made, then the last day of the due month is used.

Example: Find the due date of a 2-month loan made on July 31.

Solution:

July 31 to August 31	1 month
August 31 to September 30	1 month
	2 months

The loan is due on September 30.

The method used to count time may cause a difference of a day or two in the length of the loan, which will affect the amount of interest earned. For example, the 2-month loan in the problem above was made on July 31 and was due on September 30. By ordinary interest, the time would be counted as follows: 2 months × 30 days = 60 days. By the exact time method, the exact count of days from July 31 to September 30 would be 61 days (31 days in August plus 30 days in September).

Using the ordinary interest method, determine (a) when the following loans are due and (b) the amount of interest to be paid.

ANSWERS

11. a. ____________
    b. ____________

12. a. ____________
    b. ____________

13. a. ____________
    b. ____________

11. A loan of $1,650 is made on April 15 for 2 months at 8%.

12. A 6-month loan for $4,269 is made on August 31, 1987, at a rate of 11%.

13. Lynda Franck, credit manager for Massina Masons, has arranged for a 3-month loan to a customer of $8,575 at 14 percent interest. The loan was made on June 30. The customer wants the interest on the loan computed by the **a.** ordinary interest method, while Lynda Franck must use **b.** the exact time method. How much interest would be earned by each method?

NAME DATE

SKILL BUILDER 25B

Using a Simple Interest Table

Simple interest can be computed by using a table such as the one shown on page 137. This table shows the interest earned for $100 at various rates of interest and for different periods of time. To use the simple interest table, follow these steps.

1. Find the appropriate rate of interest column at the top of the table.

2. Find the appropriate number of days or months of interest in the Time column.

3. Locate the point at which the Rate-of-Interest column and the Time column meet. This point indicates the amount of interest earned by $100 at that rate for that period of time.

4. Divide the principal by 100 (move the decimal point two places to the left) to determine the number of $100 units contained in the principal.

5. Multiply the interest on $100 by the factor obtained in step 4 to determine the amount of interest earned.

Example: Find the interest earned on $1,729.85 for 17 days at a rate of $6\frac{1}{2}$ percent. Round off the answer to the nearest cent.

Solution: Select the $6\frac{1}{2}\%$ column, and then move down to row 17. The factor of 0.3069 is the interest earned on $100 for 17 days at $6\frac{1}{2}$ percent.

Interest	=	*Loan*	×	*Interest Factor*
?	=	$17.2985	×	0.3069
?	=	$5.3089096 →		$5.31

Computing the same interest by the interest formula method gives the following result.

$$I = P \times R \times T$$
$$? = \$1{,}729.85 \times 0.065 \times \frac{17}{360}$$
$$? = \$5.309678 \rightarrow \$5.31$$

This demonstrates that the table gives a sufficiently accurate result.

To determine the interest factor for time periods or interest rates not shown on the table, factors may be combined. The simplest combinations should always be used when combining factors.

Example: Using the simple interest table, find the interest earned on $3,000 at $10\frac{1}{2}$ percent for 72 days.

Solution: $10\frac{1}{2}\% = 4\% + 6\frac{1}{2}\%$

72 days = 2 months (60 days) + 12 days

2 months =	60 days at 4%	= 0.6667
	60 days at $6\frac{1}{2}\%$	= 1.0833
	12 days at 4%	= 0.1333
	12 days at $6\frac{1}{2}\%$	= 0.2167
	72 days at $10\frac{1}{2}\%$	= 2.1000

Interest	=	*Loan* divided by 100	×	*Interest Factor*
?	=	$30.00	×	2.100
?	=	$63.00		

Check: $\$3{,}000 \times 0.105 \times \frac{72}{360} = \$63.00$

Use the simple interest table on page 137 to compute the interest charges on the following loans. You will have to determine the exact number of days for problems 9 through 12.

1. $2,500 at 11% for 48 days

2. $1,725 at 13% for 180 days

ANSWERS

1. ____________

2. ____________

3. \$8,000 at 14% for 86 days

4. \$426 at $10\frac{1}{2}$% for 75 days

ANSWERS

3. ____________
4. ____________
5. ____________
6. ____________
7. ____________
8. ____________
9. ____________
10. ____________
11. ____________
12. ____________

5. \$800 at 8% for 112 days

6. \$2,980 at $9\frac{1}{2}$% for 99 days

7. \$15,265 at 13% for 205 days

8. \$7,458 at 12% for 141 days

9. \$3,850 at 11% from October 19, 1988, to April 17, 1989

10. \$504 at $13\frac{1}{2}$% from November 20, 1988, to March 2, 1989

11. \$8,520 at $11\frac{1}{2}$% from April 2 to June 13

12. \$402 at $15\frac{1}{2}$% from May 20 to September 9

FINDING THE PRINCIPAL, RATE, OR TIME The following chart can be used to find the formula for the principal, rate, or time.

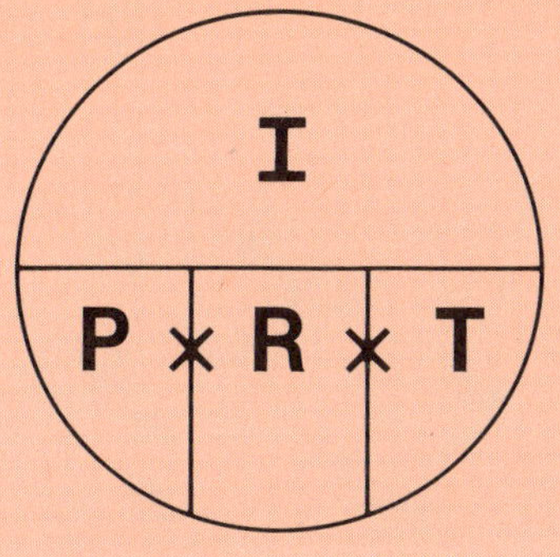

PRINCIPAL To find the principal, place a finger over the letter *P*. The remaining letters indicate that the principal may be found by dividing the interest by the product of the rate multiplied by the time.

$$P = \frac{I}{R \times T}$$

Example: If $42 interest was earned at a rate of 8 percent for 54 days, what was the amount of the loan?

Solution: The amount of the loan, or the principal, is the unknown. Change 8 percent to a decimal fraction, and substitute the known quantities in the formula.

$$P = \frac{I}{R \times T}$$

$$? = \frac{\$42}{0.08 \times \frac{54}{360}} = \frac{\$42}{0.012}$$

$$? = \$3{,}500$$

RATE To find the rate, place a finger over the letter *R* on the chart. The remaining letters indicate that the rate may be found by dividing the interest by the product of the principal multiplied by the time.

$$R = \frac{I}{P \times T}$$

Example: If $26.25 interest was earned on $3,000 for 42 days, what was the rate of interest?

Solution: The rate is the unknown. Substitute the known quantities in the formula:

$$R = \frac{I}{P \times T}$$

$$? = \frac{\$26.25}{\$3{,}000 \times \frac{42}{360}} = \frac{\$26.25}{\$350}$$

$$? = 0.075 \text{ or } 7.5\%$$

TIME To find the time, place a finger over the letter *T* on the chart. The remaining letters indicate that the time may be found by dividing the interest by the product of the principal multiplied by the rate.

$$T = \frac{I}{P \times R}$$

The resulting number represents a fraction of a year and must be multiplied by 360 to determine the number of days for which the interest was paid.

Example: For how many days was a loan outstanding if $1,750 earned $31.50 interest at a rate of 9 percent?

Solution: The time is the unknown. Substitute the known quantities in the formula.

$$T = \frac{I}{P \times R}$$

$$? = \frac{\$31.50}{\$1{,}750 \times 0.09} = \frac{\$31.50}{\$157.50}$$

$$? = 0.2 \text{ year or } 0.2 \times 360 \text{ days}$$

$$? = 72 \text{ days}$$

Solve the following problems for either the principal, the rate, or the time. Use the banker's year (360 days). Carry out all internal money amounts to 4 decimal places where necessary. Carry out percents to the nearest tenth of a percent. Round off your final answer to the nearest cent.

13. If $8.58 interest was earned at 12 percent for 60 days, what was the amount of the loan?

ANSWER

13. __________

ANSWER

14.		________
15.		________
16.		________
17.		________
18.		________
19.		________
20.		________
21.		________
22.	a.	________
	b.	________
	c.	________

14. What rate of interest was being paid if $1,250 earned $48.75 interest for 90 days?

15. For how many days was a $20,000 loan outstanding if it earned $500 interest at a rate of 10 percent?

16. How much was borrowed if interest for 96 days came to $483.98 at a rate of $10\frac{1}{2}$ percent?

17. What was the rate of interest if $50.31 interest was paid on $5,160 for 36 days?

18. For how many days was a loan outstanding if $1,050 earned $21.70 interest at a rate of $15\frac{1}{2}$ percent? Round off the fraction of a year to 4 decimal places and your final answer to the nearest whole number.

19. What was the amount of the loan if $67.15 interest was earned for 42 days at a rate of 15 percent?

20. If $5 interest was earned on $612.25 at a rate of 14 percent, for how many days was the loan outstanding? Round off the fraction of a year to 4 decimal places and your final answer to the nearest whole number.

21. Tryon Dresses was billed $39 interest on a $1,500 credit for 60 days. What rate of interest was charged?

22. Juliet Jewelry charges 18 percent interest on delinquent accounts. One customer was 42 days late in making a payment on an account of $1,815. The customer sent a check for the cost of the merchandise, plus an interest payment of $32.67.

a. Was $32.67 the correct amount of interest?

b. If not, what is the correct amount?

c. How many days did the interest payment they sent actually cover?

NAME DATE

SKILL BUILDER — Computing Exact Interest — 26A

The United States government always uses a 365-day year to compute interest. This is called **exact interest,** and it is more accurate than interest computed on a banker's year, since it is based on the true number of days in a year. To compute exact interest, use the simple interest formula $I = P \times R \times T$, but change the denominator of the time fraction from 360 to 365.

Example: Compute the exact interest due on a loan of $3,500 at 12 percent for 103 days.

Solution:

$$I = P \times R \times T$$

$$? = \$3{,}500 \times 0.12 \times \frac{103}{365}$$

$$? = \$118.520 \rightarrow \$118.52$$

Compute the exact interest due on the following loans. For most problems, it will be necessary to count the precise number of days between dates.

1. $11,000 for 180 days at 12%

2. $942 from July 10 to September 16 at $8\frac{1}{2}$%

3. $9,867 from August 20 to December 7 at $11\frac{1}{2}$%

4. $1,550 from November 14 to April 14, at 15%

5. Michele Carson, treasurer of Juliet Jewelry, has discovered an error in Juliet's tax payments. The additional $13,000 due is subject to a penalty of 25 percent of the amount owed, plus exact interest at 9 percent from April 15 to July 21, the date of the payment. What is the total amount which must be paid?

6. Pat Parker was to receive an $800 refund on his tax payment for the previous year. Because the refund was not made until June 11, he is entitled to exact interest at a rate of 8 percent from April 15 to the refund date. How much interest should he receive?

7. The First National Bank of Seattle loaned $375,000 to one of its best corporate customers. At a rate of $14\frac{1}{2}$ percent, how much interest would be earned for 32 days using the exact interest method?

8. A loan of $86,427 was made for 69 days at 13 percent interest. How much interest would be paid (a) using the banker's year method and (b) using the exact interest method?

ANSWERS

1. ____________
2. ____________
3. ____________
4. ____________
5. ____________
6. ____________
7. ____________
8. a. ____________
   b. ____________

USING A TABLE TO COMPUTE EXACT TIME The table on page 138 can be used to count the exact number of days between two dates. To use the table, follow these steps.

1. Find the month in which the loan begins in the Month Loan Begins column at the left.
2. Find the month in which the loan is due in the Month Loan Ends columns.
3. The number at the intersection of the row for the beginning month and the column for the ending month is the exact number of days between the same dates in both months.
4. If the day in the month the loan ends is later than the day in the month the loan began, add the difference in the number of days to the number found in step 3. If it is earlier, subtract the difference.

Note: The table assumes a 365-day year. If the loan period includes the month of February in a leap year, add one more day to the total number of days.

Example: What is the exact number of days between March 12 and December 12?

Solution: Since the dates are the same for both months, the answer is the number at the intersection of the row for March and the column for December: 275 days.

Example: What is the exact number of days between April 22 and July 5?

Solution:

April 22 to July 22	91 days (from table)
July 5 to July 22	− 17 days
Exact number of days	74 days

Determine the exact time and interest for the following loans, using the table on page 138 to count the days.

	AMOUNT OF LOAN	RATE	TERM OF LOAN	METHOD	NUMBER OF DAYS	INTEREST DUE
9.	$ 3,590.00	16%	8/12 to 11/9	Banker's	________	________
10.	1,527.00	15%	1/18 to 4/11 (Non-leap year)	Exact	________	________
11.	450.00	11%	12/14 to 2/28	Exact	________	________
12.	5,872.00	$13\frac{1}{2}$%	6/23 to 12/15	Banker's	________	________
13.	1,624.00	9%	4/26 to 6/12	Banker's	________	________
14.	8,527	$12\frac{3}{4}$%	1/16 to 4/10	Exact	________	________
15.	37,693	$10\frac{1}{4}$%	10/9 to 2/6	Banker's	________	________

NAME DATE

SKILL BUILDER 26B

Computing Compound Interest

When money is deposited in a savings bank or other savings institution, the account earns **compound interest.** This means that the interest made on an account is periodically combined with the principal so that the base amount on which interest is paid becomes greater and greater. To compute compound interest, follow these steps.

1. Find the simple interest on the principal for one interest period, using the simple interest formula $I = P \times R \times T$.
2. Add this interest to the first period principal to find the principal for the second period.
3. Compute the interest earned on the second period principal.
4. Add the second period interest to the second period principal to find the third period principal.
5. Repeat this procedure for each period for which compound interest is to be earned. The total of the original principal and all interest earned is the **compound amount.** To find the compound interest earned, subtract the original principal from the compound amount.

Example: $5,000 is deposited in a savings account earning interest at 8 percent compounded annually. How much would be in the account at the end of 2 years if the interest is left in the account? What is the compound interest?

Solution:

Year 1:	$5,000 × 0.08 × 1 =	$400 interest
	+400	First year's interest
Year 2:	$5,400 × 0.08 × 1 =	$432 interest
	+432	Second year's interest
	$5,832	Compound amount

$5,832	Compound amount
−5,000	Original principal
$ 832	Compound interest

A simple interest computation would have resulted in only $800 interest ($400 for each year). Interest is usually compounded more than once a year. When this happens, replace the time factor of 1 in the simple interest formula by a common fraction representing the compounding period (semiannual, $\frac{1}{2}$; quarterly, $\frac{1}{4}$; monthly, $\frac{1}{12}$; daily $\frac{1}{365}$). In the previous example, if the interest were compounded twice a year, an additional $17.29 in interest would be earned.

Period 1:	$5,000.00 × 0.08 × $\frac{1}{2}$ =	$200.00 interest
	+200.00	Interest
Period 2:	$5,200.00 × 0.08 × $\frac{1}{2}$ =	$208.00 interest
	+208.00	Interest
Period 3:	$5,408.00 × 0.08 × $\frac{1}{2}$ =	$216.32 interest
	+216.32	Interest
Period 4:	$5,624.32 × 0.08 × $\frac{1}{2}$ =	$224.97 interest
	+224.97	Interest
	$5,849.29	Compound amount

Find (a) the compound amount and (b) the compound interest for these accounts. Round off all money amounts to the nearest cent where necessary.

1. $1,500 at 6% compounded annually for 3 years

2. $6,000 at $5\frac{1}{2}$% compounded annually for 4 years.

ANSWERS

1. a. ____________
   b. ____________
2. a. ____________
   b. ____________

3. $3,000 at 7% compounded semiannually for 4 years

ANSWERS

3. a. ____________

   b. ____________

4. a. ____________

   b. ____________

4. $12,000 at 6% compounded quarterly for 2 years

Compound interest can be computed by using the rate of interest for a compounding period in the formula instead of the annual rate.

Example: $5,000 is deposited in a savings account earning interest at 8 percent compounded semiannually for one year. Find the compound amount and the compound interest.

Solution:

1. Determine the number of compounding periods in one year (semiannually = 2 periods a year).
2. Divide the annual rate of interest by the number of compounding periods in a year (8% ÷ 2 = 4%).
3. Add 1 to the period rate found in step 2 (0.04 + 1 = 1.04). When the principal on deposit is multiplied by a factor such as this, the product is the compound amount, principal plus interest, for that period.
4. Multiply the total time on deposit by the number of compounding periods in one year to determine the number of compounding computations to be made (1 year × 2 periods a year for semiannual compounding = 2 compounding periods).
5. Multiply the beginning principal by the factor obtained in step 3. Continue to multiply the resulting product by this factor for the required number of compounding periods obtained in step 4.

Period 1:

$5,000 × 1.04 = $5,200

Period 2:

$5,200 × 1.04 =	$5,408	Compound amount
	−5,000	Original principal
	$ 408	Compound interest

Using the above method, find (a) the compound amount and (b) the compound interest for these accounts. Carry out the periodic rate to 4 decimal places where necessary.

5. $850 at 6% compounded semiannually for 2 years

6. $3,600 at 5% compounded every 3 months for 2 years

7. $7,500 at 7% compounded quarterly, for three-fourths of a year

ANSWERS

5. a. ______
   b. ______
6. a. ______
   b. ______
7. a. ______
   b. ______

THE COMPOUND INTEREST TABLE The table on page 138 lists factors needed to compute compound interest at various rates for up to 25 interest compounding periods.

Example: Compute the compound amount and compound interest on $5,580 at 6 percent compounded quarterly for 5 years.

Solution:

1. Determine the number of compounding periods in one year (quarterly = 4).
2. Divide the annual rate of interest by the number of compounding periods in one year to get the interest rate per period (6% ÷ 4 = $1\frac{1}{2}$%).
3. Multiply the total time on deposit by the number of compounding periods in one year to get the total number of compounding periods (5 years × 4 = 20).
4. Locate the appropriate interest rate column in the table ($1\frac{1}{2}$%). Move down the rate column to the line matching the total number of periods determined in step 3, in this case, 20. The factor at this point is the value of $1 compounded at that rate for that period of time: 1.3469.
5. Multiply the original principal by the compound factor to get the compound amount.

Compound Amount	=	*Original Principal*	×	*Compound Factor*
?	=	$5,580	×	1.3469
?	=	$7,515.70		

$7,515.70 Compound amount
−5,580.00 Original principal
$1,935.70 Compound interest

Use the table starting on page 138 to find the compound amount and the compound interest for the following accounts. Use *four* decimal places for the compound factor.

	PRINCIPAL	ANNUAL INTEREST RATE	TIME ON DEPOSIT	COMPOUNDED	COMPOUND AMOUNT	COMPOUND INTEREST
8.	$8,000	11%	4 years	Quarterly	______	______
9.	4,100	9%	12 years	Semiannually	______	______
10.	1,260	5%	6 years	Quarterly	______	______
11.	6,975	7%	$12\frac{1}{2}$ years	Semiannually	______	______

	PRINCIPAL	ANNUAL INTEREST RATE	TIME ON DEPOSIT	COMPOUNDED	COMPOUND AMOUNT	COMPOUND INTEREST
12.	$ 7,500	12%	3 years	Quarterly	________	________
13.	12,000	6%	2 years	Quarterly	________	________
14.	4,500	15%	2 years	Monthly	________	________
15.	5,000	4%	10 years	Semiann.	________	________
16.	3,700	11%	$4\frac{1}{2}$ years	Quarterly	________	________
17.	4,000	5%	10 years	Annually	________	________
18.	4,000	$4\frac{1}{2}$%	10 years	Semiann.	________	________
19.	38,500	$8\frac{1}{4}$%	3 years	every 4 months	________	________

On page 138 is a compound interest table for daily compounding of interest. It is customary to credit the interest earned at the end of each month when interest is compounded daily. To use this table, select the appropriate annual rate column, and then read down the column to the number of days for the compounding factor.

Example: How much interest would $5,000 earn at a rate of 6 percent, compounded daily for 30 days?

Solution: Read down the 6% column to line 30. The factor is 1.0049393. Then multiply the principal by the compounding factor to find the compound amount.

$5,000 × 1.0049393 = $5,024.70 Compound amount

Subtract the original principal from the compound amount to find the compound interest.

$5,024.70	Compound amount
−5,000.00	Original principal
$ 24.70	Compound interest

Use the daily compounding table on page 138 to find the compound amount and the compound interest earned by these accounts. Use 7 decimal places for the compound factor.

	PRINCIPAL	ANNUAL INTEREST RATE	TIME ON DEPOSIT	COMPOUND AMOUNT	COMPOUND INTEREST
20.	$ 8,000	$7\frac{1}{2}$%	23 days	________	________
21.	11,500	$6\frac{1}{2}$%	31 days	________	________
22.	35,000	7%	5 days	________	________
23.	1,300	8%	29 days	________	________
24.	19,800	6%	19 days	________	________
25.	14,159	$5\frac{1}{2}$%	12 days	________	________

NAME DATE

SKILL BUILDER 27A

Discounting Noninterest-Bearing Notes and Drafts

A **promissory note** is a written promise to pay a sum of money at a specific time. The date on which the payment is promised is the **due date,** or **maturity date.** The maturity date of the note may be specified exactly, or it may be stated as a definite number of days, months, or years from the date of issue of the note. The time period from the date of issue to the maturity date is the **term of the note.**

To find the maturity date of a 60-day note dated July 20, count the exact number of days from the date of issue to determine the date on which the note is to be paid. If the term of the note is stated in months, count forward from the date of the note the given number of months to the same date in the month of maturity. For example, a 2-month note issued July 15 would be due September 15. A 2-month note issued July 31 would be due September 30, since there are only 30 days in September. If cash is needed before the maturity date of the note, the business may sell the note to a bank. This process is called **discounting the note,** and the date of sale to the bank is the **discount date.** The **term of discount** is the exact number of days from the discount date to the maturity date.

Example: Find the maturity date and term of discount of a 90-day note dated June 20 and discounted July 9.

Solution: Use the table on page 138 to determine the exact number of days between two months.

June 20 to September 20 = 92 days
Less 2 days = September 18 **Maturity date**
July 9 to September 9 = 62 days
September 9 to September 18 = 9 days
62 days + 9 days = 71 days **Term of discount**

If the same note ran for 3 months and was discounted on the same date, the maturity date would be September 20 and the term of discount from July 9 to September 20 would be 73 days.

FINDING THE PROCEEDS OF A NONINTEREST-BEARING NOTE When a note is discounted, the bank charges banker's interest, the **amount of discount.** The interest is computed on the face value for the term of discount, and is then deducted from the face value of the note. The balance, called the **proceeds** of the note, is paid to the borrower. A typical noninterest-bearing note is shown below. If this note was discounted on May 1 at 14 percent, the proceeds would be found as follows.

Face value of note	$1,500.00
Maturity date	
60 days from April 17 = June 16	
Term of discount	
May 1 to June 16 = 46 days	
Less amount of discount	
$\$1,500 \times 0.14 \times \frac{46}{360}$	26.83
Proceeds	$1,473.17

$ 1,500.00 April 17, 19 —

Sixty days after date I promise to pay to

the order of Kris Koshak

One thousand five hundred and 00/100 —— Dollars

Payable at Morgan State Bank

Value received with no interest

No. 1785 Due June 16, 19— John A. Bailey

1. Find the maturity date and term of discount for each.

	DATE OF NOTE	TERM OF NOTE	MATURITY DATE	DISCOUNT DATE	TERM OF DISCOUNT
a.	Sept. 30	30 days	________	Oct. 15	________
b.	Jan. 18, 1987	45 days	________	Jan. 31	________
c.	Mar. 31	3 months	________	May 4	________
d.	Sept. 25	120 days	________	Oct. 25	________

2. Find the maturity date, term of discount, amount of discount, and proceeds for the noninterest-bearing notes below. Use the banker's year.

	FACE VALUE	TERM OF NOTE	DATE OF NOTE	DISCOUNT DATE	RATE OF DISCOUNT	MATURITY DATE	TERM OF DISCOUNT	AMOUNT OF DISCOUNT	PROCEEDS
a.	$ 500.00	30 days	Jan. 5	Jan. 15	14%	________	________	________	________
b.	1,750.00	90 days	Mar. 26	May 2	11%	________	________	________	________
c.	5,000.00	2 months	Nov. 18	Dec. 31	$13\frac{1}{2}$%	________	________	________	________
d.	8,659.00	72 days	June 12	July 1	15%	________	________	________	________

A **draft** is a written order for payment made by one party to another. It differs from a check in that it must be accepted before it becomes legally binding. If the draft calls for payment at a specified date, it is a **time draft,** in which case the date of acceptance is not important. When the draft calls for payment a certain time after sight, or acceptance, it is a **sight draft,** and the maturity date can only be determined after the draft has been presented for acceptance. A draft is discounted in the same way as a promissory note.

Example: Find the proceeds on a sight draft for $3,850. Its maturity date is 45 days after sight. It was accepted on November 15 and discounted on December 15 at 12 percent.

Solution:

Face value of draft $3,850.00

Maturity date

45 days from Nov. 15 = Dec. 30

Term of discount

Dec. 15 to Dec. 30 = 15 days

Less amount of discount

$\$3{,}850 \times 0.12 \times \frac{15}{360}$ .... −19.25

Proceeds $3,830.75

3. Find the maturity date, term of discount, amount of discount, and proceeds for the noninterest-bearing drafts below. Use the banker's year.

	FACE VALUE	DATE OF DRAFT	DUE DATE	ACCEPTANCE DATE	DISCOUNT DATE	RATE OF DISCOUNT	MATURITY DATE	TERM OF DISCOUNT	AMOUNT OF DISCOUNT	PROCEEDS
a.	$2,000	Mar. 30	60 days from date	Apr. 15	Apr. 30	11%	________	________	________	________
b.	5,500	Sept. 12	45 days after sight	Oct. 2	Oct. 15	15%	________	________	________	________
c.	1,200	Feb. 15	3 months from date	Feb. 28	Mar. 1	13%	________	________	________	________
d.	875	Oct. 9	90 days after sight	Nov. 1	Nov. 2	11.5%	________	________	________	________

NAME DATE

SKILL BUILDER — Discounting Interest-Bearing Notes and Drafts — 27B

Promissory notes and drafts may or may not bear interest. When a borrower uses any of these as **collateral,** that is, security for a loan, the bank pays the proceeds to the borrower and collects the maturity value when the obligation is due. The **maturity value** of an interest-bearing note or draft is the face value plus interest earned for the period of the note or draft. The bank lends the maturity value less the amount of discount (interest) computed on the maturity value. The borrower receives the remainder, or **proceeds.**

Example: A $2,000 90-day promissory note, dated July 2, with interest at 14 percent is discounted on August 15 at 15 percent. Find the proceeds.

Solution:

Maturity date
90 days from July 2 = Sept. 30

Face value	$2,000.00
Plus interest: $\$2{,}000 \times 0.14 \times \frac{90}{360}$	+70.00
Maturity value	$2,070.00

Term of discount
Aug. 15 to Sept. 30 = 46 days

Less amount of discount $\$2{,}070 \times 0.15 \times \frac{46}{360}$	−39.67
Proceeds	$2,030.33

Find the proceeds for each of the following notes. Use the banker's year.

1.

	A	B	C	D	E
Face value	$1,000.00	$1,920.00	$516.00	$296.40	$5,784.00
Term of note	2 months	60 days	3 months	90 days	120 days
Rate of interest	13%	12%	14%	15%	11%
Amount of interest	______	______	______	______	______
Maturity value	______	______	______	______	______
Date of note	Nov. 5	June 19	May 30	Feb. 21, 1983	October 31
Discount date	Dec. 6	July 9	July 16	April 4	February 1
Rate of discount	14%	$14\frac{1}{2}$%	15%	17%	16%
Maturity date	______	______	______	______	______
Term of discount	____ days	____ days	____ days	____ days	____ days
Amount of discount	______	______	______	______	______
Proceeds	______	______	______	______	______

2. Lisa Hahn took a 120-day note for $1,500 from Sidney Wilde. The note was dated May 3, with interest at 12 percent. On May 18, Lisa Hahn sold the note to First Federal Bank at a discount rate of 14 percent. What were the proceeds on the note?

ANSWER

2. ______

3. Find the proceeds for each of these drafts, using the banker's year.

	A	B	C	D	E
Face value	$2,250.00	$3,840.00	$6,000.00	$1,769.00	$2,750.00
Date of draft	May 5	July 12	Aug. 8	Oct. 19	Jan. 17
When due	75 days from date	2 months after sight	3 months from date	45 days after sight	180 days from date
Acceptance date	May 12	July 21	Aug. 12	Nov. 1	Mar. 17
Rate of interest	14%	0%	$12\frac{1}{2}$%	0%	15%
Amount of interest	______	______	______	______	______
Maturity value	______	______	______	______	______
Maturity date	______	______	______	______	______
Discount date	May 15	Aug. 4	Aug. 15	Nov. 8	May 15
Rate of discount	15%	18%	16%	14%	13%
Term of discount	______ days	______ days	______ days	______ days	______ days
Amount of discount	______	______	______	______	______
Proceeds	______	______	______	______	______

Some banks may deduct a certain percent of the maturity value of the note. The amount deducted is called the **collection fee.**

Example: A 30-day, 14-percent note with a face amount of $2,000 is discounted after 10 days at a rate of 15 percent. The bank charges a 0.1% collection fee. Find the proceeds.

Solution:

Face value	$2,000.00
Plus interest: $\$2,000 \times 0.14 \times \frac{30}{360}$	+23.33
Maturity value	$2,023.33
Less collection fee: $2,023.33 × 0.001 ...	−2.02
	$2,021.31
Less discount: $\$2,023.33 \times 0.15 \times \frac{20}{360}$ ..	−16.86
Proceeds	$2,004.45

Find the proceeds using the banker's year.

ANSWERS

4. ______

5. ______

4. Melody Manufacturers was given a 120-day, noninterest-bearing note for $2,315. The note was dated July 14, and was discounted on September 1 at a rate of 18 percent. Find the proceeds.

5. Steve Zoltan held a 3-month noninterest-bearing note for $750, dated March 31. He discounted the note at his bank on April 15 at a rate of 15 percent. There is a 0.1% collection fee charged by the bank. What proceeds did Steve receive?

NAME DATE

SKILL BUILDER — Installment Purchases — 28A

Installment purchasing, or **buying on time,** is paying for an item by making a down payment, and then making a series of payments, or installments, over a specified period of time. The usual practice is to charge interest for the privilege of making an installment purchase, although sometimes an installment purchase may cost no more than a cash purchase. The installment purchaser is generally charged various fees, such as an application fee for the loan, a credit investigation fee, and an insurance fee on the amount of the loan. These are added costs of buying on time.

To find the added cost of making an installment purchase, follow these steps.

1. Multiply the number of payments by the amount of each payment.

2. Add this product to the down payment. This total will be the **total installment price.**

3. Subtract the cash purchase price from the total installment price.

The difference will be the added cost, if any, of buying on time.

Example: A color television has a cash purchase price of $450. If it is purchased on an installment plan, a down payment of $45 and 15 monthly payments of $30.26 each are required. What is the added cost, if any, of buying the television on time?

Solution:

Monthly payments: 15 × $30.26	$453.90
Plus down payment	+45.00
Total installment price	$498.90
Less cash price	−450.00
Added cost of buying on time	$48.90

Find the added cost, if any, of buying on time for each.

1.

	ITEM	INSTALLMENT TERMS: DOWN PAYMENT	NUMBER OF PAYMENTS	MONTHLY PAYMENT	INSTALLMENT PRICE	CASH PRICE	COST OF BUYING ON TIME
a.	Typewriter	none	12	$ 21.89	________	$ 240.00	________
b.	Cassette Player	$ 11.95	4	27.00	________	119.95	________
c.	Stereo	none	15	20.77	________	279.95	________
d.	Microwave	39.95	24	16.72	________	379.95	________
e.	Tent	19.99	9	18.17	________	169.99	________
f.	Refrigerator	58.00	30	21.32	________	579.95	________

2. George Manley purchased a $319.95 dish washer on an installment purchase plan. The purchase plan required a down payment of $31.95 and weekly payments of $4.25 for 78 weeks. What is the added cost of buying on time?

3. Lauren Black purchased a used car priced at $5,430. In order to purchase on the installment plan, she had to make a 20 percent down payment and pay the balance in 24 monthly payments of $221 each. How much more did it cost to buy the car on time?

ANSWERS

2. ________

3. ________

TRUTH-IN-LENDING The Truth-in-Lending Act requires that the lender state the true annual rate of interest. The rate may be stated as "$1\frac{1}{2}$% a month (18% annual rate)." This tells the borrower that a rate of 18 percent is being charged only on the amount of money actually owed.

Add-on interest assumes that the borrower owes the entire sum of money over the period of the loan because the interest charged is computed for the entire period of the loan. Since a portion of the principal is being repaid with each payment, the borrower actually has the full use of the money for only a part of the period of the loan.

Example: A typewriter with a cash purchase price of $240 is sold on the installment purchase plan with no down payment. Add-on interest at an annual rate of 10 percent is charged to the purchaser, along with an application fee of $2.20, a credit check fee of $5, and insurance at a flat rate of $\frac{1}{2}$ percent of the amount of the loan. If the typewriter is to be paid for in one year, what is the cost of buying on time, and what is the monthly payment?

Solution:

Cash price and amount of loan	$240.00
Plus interest: $240 × 0.10 × 1.	24.00
Plus application fee and credit check:	7.20
Plus insurance charge: $240 × 0.005.	+1.20
Total installment price	$272.40
Less cash price	−240.00
Added cost of buying on time	$32.40
Monthly payment: $272.40 ÷ 12.	$22.70

Neither add-on interest nor additional charges give a true picture of the real rate of interest being paid. To find the real rate of interest for the typewriter, use this formula.

$$\text{Real Rate of Interest} = \frac{2 \times 12^{*} \times \text{Added Cost of Buying on Time}}{\text{Amount of Loan} \times (\text{Number of Payments} + 1)}$$

$$? = \frac{2 \times 12 \times \$32.40}{\$240 \times (12 + 1)} = \frac{24 \times \$32.40}{\$240 \times 13}$$

$$? = \frac{\$777.60}{\$3{,}120} = 0.2492 \text{ or } 24.9\%$$

* If payments are made monthly, this number is 12.
If payments are made weekly, this number is 52.

Find the real rate of interest to the nearest tenth of a percent on these purchases.

4.

	ITEM	CASH PRICE	INSTALLMENT TERMS: DOWN PAYMENT	NUMBER OF PAYMENTS	MONTHLY PAYMENT	REAL RATE OF INTEREST
a.	Tent	$169.99	$19.99	9	$18.17	______
b.	Radio	76.50	6.50	12	6.50	______
c.	Stereo	279.95	none	15	20.77	______
d.	Microwave	379.95	39.95	24	16.72	______

NAME DATE

SKILL BUILDER 28B

Computing Interest on Unpaid Balances

Because each payment made on an installment purchase pays back a portion of the principal, the fairest basis is to base the interest on the unpaid balance.

Example: A lawn mower was purchased on April 1 for $240, less a down payment of $60. The balance of $180 is to be paid off in equal monthly installments over a period of 3 months with interest on the unpaid balance at 15 percent. Prepare a table of the installment payments and balance due each month.

Solution:

$$\text{Payment Toward Principal} = \text{Balance} \div \text{Number of Months}$$
$$? = \$180 \div 3$$
$$? = \$60$$

$$\text{Interest Rate for Month} = \frac{\text{Interest Rate for Year}}{12}$$
$$? = \frac{0.15}{12}$$
$$? = 0.0125$$

PAYMENT DATE	UNPAID BALANCE	INTEREST FOR MONTH	AMOUNT DUE	INSTALLMENT PAYMENT	BALANCE DUE
May 1	$180	$2.25	$182.25	$62.25	$120
June 1	120	1.50	121.50	61.50	60
July 1	60	0.75	60.75	60.75	–0–

The usual practice is for equal installment payments to be made over the period of the loan. To do this, the total of principal payments plus interest earned would be divided by the number of payments.

Principal payments: 3 × $60	$180.00
Plus interest owed:	
$2.25 + $1.50 + $0.75	4.50
Total	$184.50

$$\text{Monthly Payment Toward Loan} = \text{Principal and Interest Balance} \div \text{Number of Months}$$
$$? = \$184.50 \div 3$$
$$? = \$61.50$$

Find the amount due each month on the following installment sales if equal payments are made against the principal. Carry out the interest for each month to *four* decimal places.

ANSWER

1. b. __________

1. Richy Donaldson purchased a video game on the installment plan. The cash price was $159.99, less a down payment of $19.99. The balance was to be paid off over 4 months with interest at 21 percent on the unpaid balance.

a. Complete this table to determine the balance due each month.

PAYMENT NUMBER	UNPAID BALANCE	INTEREST FOR MONTH	AMOUNT DUE	INSTALLMENT PAYMENT	BALANCE DUE
1	______	______	______	______	______
2	______	______	______	______	______
3	______	______	______	______	______
4	______	______	______	______	______

b. What would the equal monthly payment for principal and interest be? (Round up your final answer to the next whole cent.)

2. Calorie Counting Cafeteria is replacing its central air conditioner at a cost of $799. After a down payment of $79, the balance will be paid in 6 monthly installments, with interest at 15 percent on the unpaid balance. What is the balance due each month?

PAYMENT NUMBER	UNPAID BALANCE	INTEREST FOR MONTH	AMOUNT DUE	INSTALLMENT PAYMENT	BALANCE DUE
1	______	______	______	______	______
2	______	______	______	______	______
3	______	______	______	______	______
4	______	______	______	______	______
5	______	______	______	______	______
6	______	______	______	______	______

A SHORTCUT FOR COMPUTING INTEREST ON UNPAID BALANCES Rather than compute the interest separately for each payment, it is possible to accomplish the same result with a formula. The interest for the lawn mower in the example on page 125 would be computed as follows.

Where the monthly payment does not work out evenly, the usual practice is to round *up* to the next whole cent. This will result in a final payment which is slightly smaller than the other payments.

$$\textit{First Month Interest} = \textit{Principal} \times \textit{Rate} \times \textit{Time}$$

$$? = \$180 \times 0.15 \times \frac{1}{12}$$

$$? = \$2.25$$

$$\textit{Interest on Unpaid Balances} = \frac{\textit{First Month Interest} \times \textit{Number of Payments} + 1}{2}$$

$$? = \frac{\$2.25 \times (3 + 1)}{2}$$

$$? = \frac{\$9.00}{2} = \$4.50$$

$$\textit{Monthly Payment Toward Loan} = \textit{Principal and Interest Balance} \div \textit{Number of Months}$$

$$? = (\$180 + \$4.50) \div 3$$

$$? = \frac{\$184.50}{3} = \$61.50$$

3. Paul Graham bought a used delivery van for $4,250. He used his old compact car valued at $250, plus $750 cash, for the down payment. The balance is to be paid in 15 equal installments with interest at 16 percent on the unpaid balance.

Compute (a) the interest on the unpaid balances and (b) the equal monthly payment for the purchase (round up your final answer to the next whole cent).

ANSWERS

3. a. ______

b. ______

NAME DATE

SKILL BUILDER — Computing Cash Discounts — 29A

A **cash discount** is a deduction allowed on money owed in order to encourage prompt payment. The rate of discount and the time period allowed to take advantage of the cash discount are called the **terms.** Assume that the terms on an invoice are 3/10, 2/30, n/60. These payment terms provide two opportunities for the buyer to take advantage of a cash discount. The expression 3/10 means that a 3 percent discount can be taken if the bill is paid within 10 days. The second expression, 2/30, means that only a 2 percent discount can be taken if payment is made 11 to 30 days after the date of the invoice. More than one cash discount period may be indicated, but only one cash discount is allowed. The expression n/60 means that payment in full is due within 60 days of the invoice date. Cash discounts are never taken on service charges, such as freight, packing, insurance, and so on. If charges of this kind are included in the invoice, they must be deducted before the cash and trade discounts are taken, and then added back in, to find the total amount due.

Example: An invoice for $1,700, dated May 28, has terms of 3/10, 2/30, n/45. What is the last date on which each cash discount can be taken? When is the net payment due? What is the amount due in each instance?

Solution: May 28 + 10 days = June 7

Amount of invoice	$1,700
Less cash discount: $1,700 × 0.03	−51
Net payment	$1,649

May 28 + 30 days = June 27

Amount of invoice	$1,700
Less cash discount: $1,700 × 0.02	−34
Net payment	$1,666

May 28 + 45 days = July 12

Amount of invoice	$1,700
No cash discount allowed after June 27	−0
Net payment	$1,700

1. Assume that these bills are paid within the cash discount period. Find the cash discount and the net payment for each invoice.

	AMOUNT OF INVOICE	TERMS	CASH DISCOUNT	NET PAYMENT
a.	$ 875.00	5/20, n/30	______	______
b.	1,658.00	3/10, n/30	______	______
c.	2,893.51	2/15, n/45	______	______

2. Find the cash discount, if any, and the net payment for these invoices.

	AMOUNT OF INVOICE	TERMS	DATE OF INVOICE	DATE OF PAYMENT	CASH DISCOUNT	NET PAYMENT
a.	$3,800.00	3/10, n/30	Oct. 13	Oct. 16	______	______
b.	1,725.30	2/10, 1/30, n/60	Nov. 20	Dec. 7	______	______
c.	5,167.51	10/10, 3/30, n/60	June 15	July 16	______	______
d.	2,950.00	8/10, 4/30, n/60	Mar. 23	Apr. 24	______	______

Cash discount periods are sometimes counted from the end of the month in which the invoice is dated (EOM = End of Month) or after the merchandise has been received (ROG = Receipt of Goods).

Example: The terms on an invoice dated May 21 are 2/10, n/30 EOM. What is the last date on which the 2 percent cash discount can be taken, and what is the date for net payment?

Solution: The cash discount period runs from May 21 to 10 days after the end of the month: June 10. Net payment is due June 30.

Example: Terms on an invoice dated August 10 are 3/15, n/45 ROG. The shipment was received on September 29. What is the last date on which the 3 percent cash discount can be taken, and what is the date for net payment?

Solution: Since the goods were received on September 29, the discount can be taken for 15 days after that date, or until October 14. Net payment is due November 13.

3. Find the discount period, the cash discount, if any, and the net payment for these invoices.

	DATE OF INVOICE	TERMS	DATE GOODS RECEIVED	DATE OF PAYMENT	DISCOUNT PERIOD	AMOUNT OF INVOICE	CASH DISCOUNT	NET PAYMENT
a.	Nov. 21	2/10, n/30 EOM	Nov. 23	Dec. 8	______	$ 727.80	______	______
b.	Sept. 16	3/15, n/30 EOM	Sept. 22	Oct. 14	______	1,464.00	______	______
c.	June 6	3/10, n/30 ROG	June 12	June 20	______	2,748.00	______	______
d.	Dec. 11	4/10, n/30 ROG	Dec. 18	Dec. 20	______	482.00	______	______
e.	Jan. 6	2/10, n/30 EOM	Jan. 20	Feb. 5	______	4,226.10	______	______
f.	Aug. 19	1/10, n/30 EOM	Aug. 30	Sept. 11	______	864.80	______	______

4. Jameson Products received a shipment of electronic parts on October 25. The invoice, in the amount of $985.50, was dated October 20. The cash discount terms were 3/10, n/45 EOM.
a. What is the last day on which a cash discount may be taken?
b. What amount must be paid then?

5. A shipment invoiced at $3,650 was received by Gable Inc. on May 17. The invoice was dated April 29, with terms of 3/10, n/30 ROG. If payment is made on May 26, how much would Gable Inc. pay?

6. In the previous problem, if the invoiced amount of $3,650 included shipping charges of $112.50, insurance charges of $36.50, and special packing charges of $25, how much would Gable Inc. pay on May 26?

ANSWERS

4. a. ______
b. ______
5. ______
6. ______

NAME DATE

SKILL BUILDER 29B

Trade and Cash Discount Applications

COMPUTING TRADE DISCOUNTS The price at which an article is sold is the **list price** or **catalog price.** A **trade discount** is a deduction from the list price of an article. A trade discount is offered to qualified purchasers, such as retailers or others who purchase in large quantities. The cost to the retailer after the trade discount is taken is the **net price.**

The discount is expressed as a percent, for example, 15 percent off the list price. A series of discounts may be offered. When computing the amount of a series of trade discounts, the order in which the discounts are applied will not affect the results.

Example: What is the net price of a stereo with a list price of $380, less trade discounts of 10 percent and 5 percent?

Solution: *First Trade Discount* = *List Price* × *First Trade Discount Rate*

? = $380 × 0.10

? = $38

$380	List price
−38	First trade discount
$342	Discounted price

Second Trade Discount = *Discounted Price* × *Second Trade Discount Rate*

? = $342 × 0.05

? = $17.10

$342.00	Discounted price
−17.10	Second trade discount
$324.90	Net price

1. Find the trade discount and net price for the following.

		TRADE DISCOUNT	NET PRICE
a.	$50 less 20%	______	______
b.	$180 less 25% and 15%	______	______
c.	$900 less 48% and 22%	______	______

2. Find the trade discount, net price, cash discount, if any, and net payment for these purchases.

	LIST PRICE	TRADE DISCOUNT ALLOWED	TERMS OF INVOICE	DATE OF INVOICE	DATE GOODS RECEIVED	DATE OF PAYMENT	TRADE DISCOUNT	NET PRICE	CASH DISCOUNT	NET PAYMENT
a.	$2,873	10%, 10%	10/10, n/30	Apr. 6	Apr. 11	Apr. 16				
b.	2,400	10%, 20%	3/15, 1/30, n/60	Feb. 29	Mar. 5	Mar. 24				
c.	1,860	25%, $12\frac{1}{2}$%	5/30, n/60	Mar. 30	Apr. 15	Apr. 30				
d.	5,380	20%, 5%	3/10, n/30 EOM	Nov. 18	Nov. 19	Dec. 5				

3. Toby Tools sold and invoiced the following lot of merchandise on May 10, with terms of 6/10, 2/30, n/45 and subject to trade discounts of $7\frac{1}{2}$ percent and 5 percent. In addition there are trucking charges of $27.50. How much does the customer pay if the shipment is paid in full on May 21? Round off money amounts to the nearest cent where necessary.

5 boxes clamps @ $44.40/box
18 boxes 3″ nails @ $15.00/box
4 boxes 2″ screws @ $21.00/box
7 boxes washers @ $18.00/box
2 boxes sandpaper @ $2.63/box

ANSWERS

3. ____________
4. ____________
5. ____________
6. ____________
7. ____________
8. a. ____________
   b. ____________

4. A shipment of sporting goods was received by Athlete's Country on March 13. The invoice was dated February 26, with terms of 3/15, n/30 ROG. The shipment was billed at $3,762, including freight charges of $146.85 and insurance of $35.62. If payment is made on March 27, how much will Athlete's Country pay? Round off money amounts to the nearest cent where necessary.

5. Milco Inc. received a shipment on May 17. The invoice, dated May 13, indicated a list price of $1,800, subject to trade discounts of 20 and 10 percent. The terms of the invoice are 2/10, n/30. Additional charges include shipping at $35 and insurance at $7.50. If payment is made on May 20, how much will Limco Inc. pay?

6. Nadine Blanchard paid $500 for a canoe after a $33\frac{1}{3}$ percent trade discount had been deducted from the list price. What was the list price of the canoe? Round off percent to the nearest hundredth of a percent.

7. Radner Radiators normally grants trade discounts of 20 percent and 25 percent. By mistake, a customer was billed $1,352 after a 45 percent discount had been allowed. How much should the customer have been billed?

8. Water skis are offered for sale by two different suppliers. Deep Six has its priced at $590, less a 20 percent trade discount, with terms of 5/10, n/30. Water World has its priced at $625, less a 20 percent trade discount with terms of 10/10, n/30.

a. Which supplier offers the better price, if all cash and trade discounts are taken?

b. How much will be saved?

NAME DATE

SKILL BUILDER 30A

Changing a Discount Series to a Single-Discount Equivalent

SINGLE-DISCOUNT EQUIVALENT A series of discounts can be converted to a single discount that is equivalent to the discount series. A **single-discount equivalent** is particularly useful when the same series of discounts is used frequently. The single-discount equivalent is *not* the sum of the original discounts because each discount after the first one is based on the **remainder** after the previous discount has been deducted.

Example: Determine the single-discount equivalent of the series 20%, 10%, and 5%.

Solution: To find the single-discount equivalent, subtract each discount rate from 100%. Then find the product of these differences.

$$\begin{array}{r} 100\% \\ -20\% \\ \hline 80\% \end{array} \times \begin{array}{r} 100\% \\ -10\% \\ \hline 90\% \end{array} \times \begin{array}{r} 100\% \\ -5\% \\ \hline 95\% \end{array} = 68.4\%$$

Finally, subtract the result from 100% to get the single-discount equivalent.

100% − 68.4% = 31.6% single-discount equivalent

Find the single-discount equivalent for each series discount. Round off decimals to four decimal places, where necessary.

1. 30%, 20%, 10%
2. 25%, 10%
3. 15%, 25%, 5%, 10%
4. $33\frac{1}{3}$%, 15%, 5%
5. 50%, $12\frac{1}{2}$%, $6\frac{1}{4}$%
6. 40%, 20%, 10%
7. 60%, 30%, 15%
8. 15%, $7\frac{1}{2}$%, 5%
9. 40%, 15%, $2\frac{1}{2}$%, 10%
10. 35%, 15%, 5%, 40%, 10%

ANSWERS

1. ____________
2. ____________
3. ____________
4. ____________
5. ____________
6. ____________
7. ____________
8. ____________
9. ____________
10. ____________

NET PRICE The **net price** is the amount to be charged for an item after all discounts have been applied. To find the net price, the discounts can be subtracted from the list price or a table such as the one shown below can be used. The horizontal and vertical rate columns list different discounts. Because the order in which discounts are taken does not affect the total discount, there may be several different ways to find the net of $1 (the net price of an article that originally cost $1).

For example, the discount series 10%, 5%, and 2½% can be found in two ways. Read down the left hand rate column until two of the rates in the series are found. If the 5–2½% row is used, read across this row to the third rate in the series, 10%. The net of $1 for this series is 0.8336. Or, read down further on the left hand column to the 10–2½% row. Read across this row to the 5% column. The net of $1 is also 0.8336. After the net of $1 is found, multiply it by the total price of the goods purchased to find the net price.

Example: An item with a list price of $320 is subject to discounts of 10%, 20%, and 2½%. Find the single-discount equivalent for the item and the net price.

Solution: Read down the rate column until two of the discount rates in the series are found: 10–2½%. Read across this row to the 20% column. The factor at the intersection of this column and row is 0.702, which means that for each dollar subject to discounts of 10%, 20%, and 2½%, only $0.702 would be paid. Multiply this factor (0.702) by the total price ($320). The net price is $224.64. To find the single discount equivalent, change 0.702 to a percent and subtract it from 100%.

100% − 70.2% = 29.8% single-discount equivalent

or

100%	100%	100%
− 10%	− 20%	− 2½%
90% ×	80% ×	97½% = 70.2% Net factor

100% − 70.2% = 29.8% Single-discount equivalent

$320 × 70.2% = $224.64 Net price

or

$320.00 × 10% = $32.00
− 32.00
$288.00 × 20% = $57.60
− 57.60
$230.40 × 2½% = $5.76
− 5.76
$224.64 Net price

Any one of the above methods can be used to find the net price when a series of discounts is given.

DISCOUNT TABLE, SHOWING NET OF $1 AFTER DISCOUNTS, SHOWN AT TOP AND SIDE, ARE TAKEN OFF

RATE	5%	7½%	10%	15%	20%	25%	30%	33⅓%	40%	50%
2%	0.931	0.9065	0.882	0.833	0.784	0.735	0.686	0.6534	0.588	0.49
2½%	0.9263	0.9019	0.8775	0.8288	0.78	0.7313	0.6825	0.65	0.585	0.4875
5%	0.9025	0.8788	0.855	0.8075	0.76	0.7125	0.665	0.6334	0.57	0.475
5–2½%	0.8799	0.8568	0.8336	0.7873	0.741	0.6947	0.6484	0.6175	0.5558	0.4631
7½%	0.8788	0.8556	0.8325	0.7863	0.74	0.6938	0.6475	0.6167	0.555	0.4625
7½–5%	0.8348	0.8128	0.7909	0.7469	0.703	0.6591	0.6151	0.5859	0.5273	0.4394
10%	0.855	0.8325	0.81	0.765	0.72	0.675	0.63	0.60	0.54	0.45
10–2½%	0.8336	0.8117	0.7898	0.7459	0.702	0.6581	0.6143	0.585	0.5265	0.4388
10–5%	0.8123	0.7909	0.7695	0.7268	0.684	0.6413	0.5985	0.57	0.513	0.4275
10–5–2½%	0.7919	0.7711	0.7503	0.7086	0.6669	0.6252	0.5835	0.5558	0.5002	0.4168
10–10%	0.7695	0.7493	0.729	0.6885	0.648	0.6075	0.567	0.54	0.486	0.405
10–10–5%	0.7310	0.7118	0.6926	0.6541	0.6156	0.5771	0.5387	0.513	0.4617	0.3848
20–5%	0.722	0.703	0.684	0.646	0.608	0.57	0.532	0.5067	0.456	0.38
20–10%	0.684	0.666	0.648	0.612	0.576	0.54	0.504	0.48	0.432	0.36
25%	0.7125	0.6938	0.675	0.6375	0.60	0.5625	0.5250	0.50	0.45	0.375
25–5%	0.6769	0.6591	0.6413	0.6056	0.57	0.5344	0.4988	0.475	0.4275	0.3563
25–10%	0.6413	0.6244	0.6075	0.5738	0.54	0.5063	0.4725	0.45	0.405	0.3375
25–10–5%	0.6092	0.5932	0.5771	0.5451	0.513	0.4809	0.4489	0.4275	0.3848	0.3206

Use the table shown on page 132 to find the single-discount equivalent for each discount series.

	DISCOUNT SERIES	SINGLE-DISCOUNT EQUIVALENT
11.	25%, $7\frac{1}{2}$%	____________
12.	15%, 10%, 5%, $2\frac{1}{2}$%	____________
13.	10%, 40%, 10%, 5%	____________
14.	50%, 25%	____________
15.	10%, 5%, 10%	____________
16.	$7\frac{1}{2}$%, 5%, $7\frac{1}{2}$%	____________
17.	$33\frac{1}{3}$%, 10%, 5%, $2\frac{1}{2}$%	____________
18.	25%, 40%, 5%	____________
19.	40%, 10%, 5%, $2\frac{1}{2}$%	____________
20.	$33\frac{1}{3}$%, 10%, 5%, 25%	____________

NAME DATE

SKILL BUILDER 30B

Application of Single-Discount Equivalents

Using any of the methods shown in Skill Builder 30a, find the amount to be paid on the following purchases. Show each series discount as a single-discount equivalent. Round off percents to the nearest hundredth where necessary.

ANSWERS

1. a. ________
   b. ________
2. a. ________
   b. ________
3. a. ________
   b. ________

1. Music Land is allowed a discount of 20% and 30% on all brass instruments purchased from Sound Electronics. Six trumpets and three cornets were purchased and invoiced on August 29 at a list price of $425 each. The terms of the invoice are 10/10, n/60. The invoice was paid on September 8.

a. What is the single-discount equivalent of 20% and 30%?

b. What was the amount of the net payment?

2. A portable tape player has a list price of $150 with trade discounts of $33\frac{1}{3}$%, 10%, and $2\frac{1}{2}$%. The terms of the invoice are 5/10, n/60. The invoice is dated April 29 and is paid on May 9.

a. What is the single-discount equivalent?

b. What is the dealer's net payment for the tape player?

3. A 10-speed bicycle which retails for $185 was purchased by a dealer with trade discounts of $33\frac{1}{3}$%, 25%, and 5%. The special order was invoiced to the dealer on February 28, 1985, with terms of 5/10, 2/30, n/60. It was paid on March 10.

a. What is the single-discount equivalent?

b. What was the dealer's cost for the bicycle?

4. State Hardware Inc. shipped a quantity of merchandise to Wilder Wares on July 23. The shipment was invoiced at $610 subject to trade discounts of 25%, 5%, and $2\frac{1}{2}$%. The terms of the invoices were 3/10, n/30.

a. Find the single-discount equivalent.

b. If the shipment was paid for when it arrived on August 3, what was the amount paid?

5. Clothes Horse paid $129.60 a dozen for men's shirts after discounts of 25% and 20% had been taken. What is the list price of each shirt?

6. A moped was invoiced to Bikes, Inc. on July 25 with trade discounts of 25% and 10%. The list price was $700, and the terms of payment were 5/10, n/30. What was the amount which the dealer paid on August 5?

7. A sofa retails for $1,050. It is billed to Contemporary Furniture on May 27 with trade discounts of 20%, 10%, and 10%, and terms of 5/10, 2/30, n/90. How much did Contemporary pay for the sofa on June 7?

8. Jean's-N-Things received its fall shipment of designer jeans on September 2. The shipment was priced at $3,150, subject to trade discounts of 25%, 10%, 5%, and $2\frac{1}{2}$%, and with terms of 10/20, n/60. The invoice was dated August 30. How much was paid for the jeans on September 30?

9. The trade discount on a lot of 100 ties amounted to $325, based on discounts of 25% and 10%. What is the list price of each tie?

10. The list price of a shipment of tennis racquets was $1,354. The purchase was invoiced on March 14 with trade discounts of 20%, 10%, and 10%, and terms of 10/10,3/30, n/90. What was the amount paid on April 13?

ANSWERS

4. a. ____________

b. ____________

5. ____________

6. ____________

7. ____________

8. ____________

9. ____________

10. ____________

SIMPLE INTEREST TABLE

$100 ON A 360-DAY BASIS

TIME	2½%	3%	3½%	4%	4½%	5%	5½%	6%	6½%	7%
1 day	.0069	.0083	.0097	.0111	.0125	.0139	.0153	.0167	.0181	.0194
2 days	.0139	.0167	.0194	.0222	.0250	.0278	.0306	.0333	.0361	.0389
3 days	.0208	.0250	.0292	.0333	.0375	.0417	.0458	.0500	.0542	.0583
4 days	.0278	.0333	.0389	.0444	.0500	.0556	.0611	.0667	.0722	.0778
5 days	.0347	.0417	.0486	.0556	.0625	.0694	.0764	.0833	.0903	.0972
6 days	.0417	.0500	.0583	.0667	.0750	.0833	.0917	.1000	.1083	.1167
7 days	.0486	.0583	.0681	.0778	.0875	.0972	.1069	.1167	.1264	.1361
8 days	.0556	.0667	.0778	.0889	.1000	.1111	.1222	.1333	.1444	.1556
9 days	.0625	.0750	.0875	.1000	.1125	.1250	.1375	.1500	.1625	.1750
10 days	.0694	.0833	.0972	.1111	.1250	.1389	.1528	.1667	.1806	.1944
11 days	.0764	.0917	.1069	.1222	.1375	.1528	.1681	.1833	.1986	.2139
12 days	.0833	.1000	.1167	.1333	.1500	.1667	.1833	.2000	.2167	.2333
13 days	.0903	.1083	.1264	.1444	.1625	.1806	.1986	.2167	.2347	.2528
14 days	.0972	.1167	.1361	.1556	.1750	.1944	.2139	.2333	.2528	.2722
15 days	.1042	.1250	.1458	.1667	.1875	.2083	.2292	.2500	.2708	.2917
16 days	.1111	.1333	.1556	.1778	.2000	.2222	.2444	.2667	.2889	.3111
17 days	.1181	.1417	.1653	.1889	.2125	.2361	.2597	.2833	.3069	.3306
18 days	.1250	.1500	.1750	.2000	.2250	.2500	.2750	.3000	.3250	.3500
19 days	.1319	.1583	.1847	.2111	.2375	.2639	.2903	.3167	.3431	.3694
20 days	.1389	.1667	.1944	.2222	.2500	.2778	.3056	.3333	.3611	.3889
21 days	.1458	.1750	.2042	.2333	.2625	.2917	.3208	.3500	.3792	.4083
22 days	.1528	.1833	.2139	.2444	.2750	.3056	.3361	.3667	.3972	.4278
23 days	.1597	.1917	.2236	.2556	.2875	.3194	.3514	.3833	.4153	.4472
24 days	.1667	.2000	.2333	.2667	.3000	.3333	.3667	.4000	.4333	.4667
25 days	.1736	.2083	.2431	.2778	.3125	.3472	.3819	.4167	.4514	.4861
26 days	.1806	.2167	.2528	.2889	.3250	.3611	.3972	.4333	.4694	.5056
27 days	.1875	.2250	.2625	.3000	.3375	.3750	.4125	.4500	.4875	.5250
28 days	.1944	.2333	.2722	.3111	.3500	.3889	.4278	.4667	.5056	.5444
29 days	.2014	.2417	.2819	.3222	.3625	.4028	.4431	.4833	.5236	.5639
1 month	.2083	.2500	.2917	.3333	.3750	.4167	.4583	.5000	.5417	.5833
2 months	.4167	.5000	.5833	.6667	.7500	.8333	.9167	1.0000	1.0833	1.1667
3 months	.6230	.7500	.8750	1.0000	1.1250	1.2500	1.3750	1.5000	1.6250	1.7500
4 months	.8333	1.0000	1.1667	1.3333	1.5000	1.6667	1.8333	2.0000	2.1667	2.3333
5 months	1.0417	1.2500	1.4583	1.6667	1.8750	2.0833	2.2917	2.5000	2.7083	2.9160
6 months	1.2500	1.5000	1.7500	2.0000	2.2500	2.5000	2.7500	3.0000	3.2500	3.5070

FINDING THE EXACT NUMBER OF DAYS FROM ANY DAY IN ONE MONTH TO THE SAME DAY IN ANY OTHER MONTH

MONTH LOAN BEGINS	MONTH LOAN ENDS											
	JAN.	FEB.	MAR.	APR.	MAY	JUNE	JULY	AUG.	SEPT.	OCT.	NOV.	DEC.
Jan.	365	31	59	90	120	151	181	212	243	273	304	334
Feb.	334	365	28	59	89	120	150	181	212	242	273	303
Mar.	306	337	365	31	61	92	122	153	184	214	245	275
Apr.	275	306	334	365	30	61	91	122	153	183	214	244
May	245	276	304	335	365	31	61	92	123	153	184	214
June	214	245	273	304	334	365	30	61	92	122	153	183
July	184	215	243	274	304	335	365	31	62	92	123	153
Aug.	153	184	212	243	273	304	334	365	31	61	92	122
Sept.	122	153	181	212	242	273	303	334	365	30	61	91
Oct.	92	123	151	182	212	243	273	304	335	365	31	61
Nov.	61	92	120	151	181	212	242	273	304	334	365	30
Dec.	31	62	90	121	151	182	212	243	274	304	335	365

COMPOUND INTEREST TABLE

$1 COMPOUNDED DAILY FOR A 365-DAY YEAR

DAY	5½%	6%	6½%	7%	7½%	8%
1	1.0001506	1.0001643	1.0001780	1.0001917	1.0002054	1.0002191
2	1.0003012	1.0003286	1.0003560	1.0003834	1.0004108	1.0004382
3	1.0004518	1.0004929	1.0005340	1.0005751	1.0006162	1.0006573
4	1.0006024	1.0006572	1.0007120	1.0007669	1.0008217	1.0008765
5	1.0007530	1.0008216	1.0008901	1.0009587	1.0010272	1.0010957
6	1.0009037	1.0009860	1.0010682	1.0011505	1.0012328	1.0013150
7	1.0010540	1.0011504	1.0012463	1.0013424	1.0014384	1.0015343
8	1.0012051	1.0013148	1.0014245	1.0015343	1.0016440	1.0017537
9	1.0013558	1.0014793	1.0016027	1.0017262	1.0018497	1.0019731
10	1.0015066	1.0016438	1.0017809	1.0019182	1.0020554	1.0021926
11	1.0016574	1.0018083	1.0019592	1.0021102	1.0022612	1.0024121
12	1.0018082	1.0019728	1.0021375	1.0023023	1.0024670	1.0026317
13	1.0019590	1.0021374	1.0023158	1.0024944	1.0026729	1.0028513
14	1.0021098	1.0023020	1.0024942	1.0026865	1.0028788	1.0030710
15	1.0022607	1.0024666	1.0026726	1.0028787	1.0030847	1.0032907
16	1.0024116	1.0026313	1.0028510	1.0030709	1.0032907	1.0035105
17	1.0025625	1.0027960	1.0030295	1.0032631	1.0034967	1.0037303
18	1.0027134	1.0029607	1.0032080	1.0034554	1.0037028	1.0039502
19	1.0028644	1.0031254	1.0033865	1.0036477	1.0039089	1.0041701
20	1.0030154	1.0032902	1.0035651	1.0038400	1.0041151	1.0043901
21	1.0031664	1.0034550	1.0037437	1.0040324	1.0043213	1.0046101
22	1.0033174	1.0036198	1.0039223	1.0042248	1.0045275	1.0048302
23	1.0034684	1.0037846	1.0041009	1.0044173	1.0047338	1.0050503
24	1.0036195	1.0039495	1.0042796	1.0046098	1.0049401	1.0052705
25	1.0037706	1.0041144	1.0044583	1.0048023	1.0051465	1.0054907
26	1.0039217	1.0042793	1.0046370	1.0049949	1.0053529	1.0057110
27	1.0040728	1.0044443	1.0048158	1.0051875	1.0055593	1.0059313
28	1.0042240	1.0046093	1.0049946	1.0053801	1.0057658	1.0061516
29	1.0043752	1.0047743	1.0051734	1.0055728	1.0059723	1.0063720
30	1.0045264	1.0049393	1.0053523	1.0057655	1.0061789	1.0065924
31	1.0046776	1.0051044	1.0055312	1.0059583	1.0063855	1.0068129

PERIODS	$1\frac{1}{4}\%$	$1\frac{1}{2}\%$	2%	$2\frac{1}{4}\%$	$2\frac{1}{2}\%$	$2\frac{3}{4}\%$	3%	$3\frac{1}{2}\%$	4%	$4\frac{1}{2}\%$	5%	PERIODS
1	1.0125	1.0150	1.0200	1.0225	1.0250	1.0275	1.0300	1.0350	1.0400	1.0450	1.0600	1
2	1.0252	1.0302	1.0404	1.0455	1.0506	1.0558	1.0609	1.0712	1.0816	1.0920	1.1236	2
3	1.0380	1.0457	1.0612	1.0690	1.0769	1.0848	1.0927	1.1087	1.1249	1.1412	1.1576	3
4	1.0509	1.0614	1.0824	1.0931	1.1038	1.1146	1.1255	1.1475	1.1699	1.1925	1.2155	4
5	1.0641	1.0773	1.1041	1.1177	1.1314	1.1453	1.1593	1.1877	1.2167	1.2462	1.2763	5
6	1.0774	1.0934	1.1262	1.1428	1.1597	1.1768	1.1941	1.2293	1.2653	1.3023	1.3401	6
7	1.0909	1.1098	1.1487	1.1685	1.1887	1.2091	1.2299	1.2723	1.3159	1.3609	1.4071	7
8	1.1045	1.1265	1.1717	1.1948	1.2184	1.2424	1.2668	1.3168	1.3686	1.4221	1.4775	8
9	1.1183	1.1434	1.1951	1.2217	1.2489	1.2765	1.3048	1.3629	1.4233	1.4861	1.5513	9
10	1.1323	1.1605	1.2190	1.2492	1.2801	1.3117	1.3439	1.4106	1.4802	1.5330	1.6289	10
11	1.1464	1.1779	1.2434	1.2773	1.3121	1.3477	1.3842	1.4600	1.5395	1.6229	1.7103	11
12	1.1608	1.1956	1.2682	1.3060	1.3449	1.3848	1.4258	1.5111	1.6010	1.6959	1.7959	12
13	1.1753	1.2136	1.2936	1.3354	1.3785	1.4229	1.4685	1.5640	1.6651	1.7722	1.8856	13
14	1.1900	1.2318	1.3195	1.3655	1.4130	1.4620	1.5126	1.6187	1.7317	1.8519	1.9799	14
15	1.2048	1.2502	1.3459	1.3962	1.4483	1.5022	1.5580	1.6753	1.8009	1.9353	2.0789	15
16	1.2199	1.2690	1.3728	1.4276	1.4845	1.5435	1.6047	1.7340	1.8730	2.0224	2.1829	16
17	1.2351	1.2880	1.4002	1.4597	1.5216	1.5860	1.6528	1.7947	1.9479	2.1134	2.2920	17
18	1.2506	1.3063	1.4282	1.4926	1.5597	1.6296	1.7024	1.8575	2.0258	2.2085	2.4066	18
19	1.2662	1.3270	1.4568	1.5262	1.5987	1.6744	1.7535	1.9225	2.1068	2.3079	2.5270	19
20	1.2820	1.3469	1.4859	1.5605	1.6387	1.7204	1.8061	1.9898	2.1911	2.4117	2.6533	20
21	1.2981	1.3671	1.5157	1.5956	1.6796	1.7677	1.8603	2.0594	2.2788	2.5202	2.7860	21
22	1.3143	1.3876	1.5460	1.6315	1.7216	1.8164	1.9161	2.1315	2.3699	2.6337	2.9253	22
23	1.3307	1.4084	1.5769	1.6682	1.7646	1.8663	1.9736	2.2061	2.4647	2.7522	3.0715	23
24	1.3474	1.4295	1.6084	1.7085	1.8087	1.9176	2.0328	2.2833	2.5633	2.8760	3.2251	24
25	1.3642	1.4509	1.6406	1.7441	1.8539	1.9704	2.0938	2.3632	2.6658	3.0054	3.3864	25